8

SCENE DESIGN

A Guide to the Stage

written and illustrated by

HENNING NELMS

Dover Publications, Inc., New York

Published in Canada by General Publishing Company, Ltd., 30 Lesmill Road, Don Mills, Toronto, Ontario.

This Dover edition, first published in 1975, is an unabridged republication of the work originally published in 1970. It is reprinted by special arrangement with Sterling Publishing Co., Inc., 419 Park Avenue South, New York, New York 10016, publishers of the original edition.

International Standard Book Number: 0-486-23153-4
Library of Congress Catalog Card Number: 74-25249

Manufactured in the United States of America
Dover Publications, Inc.
180 Varick Street
New York, N.Y. 10014

CONTENTS

BEFORE YOU BEGIN

Anyone interested in studying design will do well to start with stage scenery. You can probably learn the principles of design with less effort when you work with scenery than if you start in any other field. All designs are based on the same principles. You must understand these before you will be able to create a wrist watch, an evening gown, or a setting for the theatre.

Most kinds of design require an ability to draw. Drawing is a great help in designing sets, but it is *not* essential—you can make models instead. Furthermore, model scenes of the type you need are easy to make, they take little time, and the materials used are inexpensive and readily available. If you add furniture and other PROPERTIES, or PROPS, these may

demand more skill. However, no part of a model set involves any real difficulty.

Other types of design call for a great deal of technical knowledge. Most scenery requires very little. Almost any set that could be built by high school students is technically simple.

Student designs in other fields are often mere classroom exercises, and are rarely turned into real objects. Scene designs, however, may serve for school plays, miniature theatres (Illus. 1), seasonal decorations, marionettes (Illus. 2), shadow boxes (Illus. 3), and rooms in dolls' houses. They can also be used as backgrounds for displays and models that range from tin soldiers to toy railroads. Designing is much more fun when you know that it will serve a real purpose.

Illus. 1. SET FOR MINIATURE THEATRE. The characters in this model nativity scene are cut out of stiff paper or cardboard. They are then attached to flat sticks so that they can be shoved on to the stage. With a little ingenuity, some of them can be pivoted and made to move with threads or wires. The stars are scraps of aluminium foil sewed or glued to the backdrop. The same design could be used for a Christmas decoration, a puppet play, or a scene built for live actors.

Illus. 2. ROMANTIC EXTERIOR FOR MARIONETTES. The audience can see at a glance that the play will be either a love story or a fairy tale. A design for marionettes must not include any scenery that will interfere with the strings. The balcony entrance has no top. The overhead foliage consists of two flat pieces of cardboard or cloth called borders. One is hung close to the curtain. The other must be well behind the garden wall. This set would be easy to make for marionettes, but a life-sized version would be a major undertaking. Walls which are curved or which must bear weight spell serious trouble for the scene builder.

Functions of Design

Paintings and statues are judged by eye. If they are beautiful, most people will admire them. This is not true of design. The shadow box in Illus. 3 might make a pleasant wall decoration if it were attractively painted. However, as Illus. 4 demonstrates, it would be a very limited set for a play.

There are even times when beauty can spoil a design. A scene laid in the home of a woman noted for her poor taste could not afford to be beautiful. It would miss the whole point of the play. Also, comedies cease to be funny if the background is too beautiful. I learned this the hard way when I staged a fast, wise-cracking comedy and let my designer provide a lovely set in soft tones of pink and blue. An audience looking at such a scene is no more inclined to laugh than a congregation in a church would be.

Although a designer need not always aim at beauty as most artists do, his designs are expected to meet practical requirements that the artist rarely has to face. *A setting must suit the play.* It should create the strongest possible effect with the least effort and expense. It is worthless if it fails to fit the stage on which it is to be used.

Scenery for the Play

It is obvious that sets like those in Illus. 1 and Illus. 2 would be unsatisfactory for scenes laid in modern living rooms. But you may not realize that you cannot design a "living-room set" and expect it to suit any play which calls for a living room. Actually, *each set must be designed for a particular scene in a particular play.* The better it suits that play, the less likely it is to work for any other play.

The Set as a Machine. Although a set like the one in Illus. 3 and Illus. 4 might provide an appropriate background for a certain play, directors and actors would find it a problem. There is hardly room for the actors to move, and almost any group they form would be both ineffective and unnatural. The revised version in Illus. 5 and Illus. 6 is much more practical. You can learn a great deal about scene design by making a detailed comparison of the plans in Illus. 4 and Illus. 5.

Think of each setting as a kind of machine devised to make the action of the play appear easy and natural. Every play requires a different arrangement. The plans in Illus. 5 and Illus. 7 are both interiors, but neither would fit the action of the play for which the other was designed.

Illus. 3. SHADOW BOX. This is a miniature set framed like a picture and used as a wall decoration. The atmosphere is warm, cheerful, and homelike. A life-sized version would make a good background for a comedy about pleasant people.

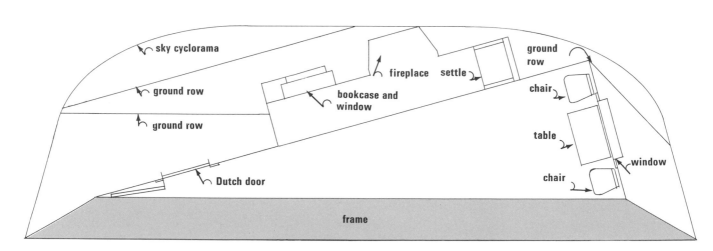

Illus. 4. FLOOR PLAN OF SHADOW BOX IN ILLUS. 3.
A design may make an appropriate background without being practical for actors. The plan shows that a stage set like this would be much too shallow. The only door is in an awkward position. Anyone seated on the settle would be hidden from the audience. The furniture is not arranged to let actors sit and talk to each other.

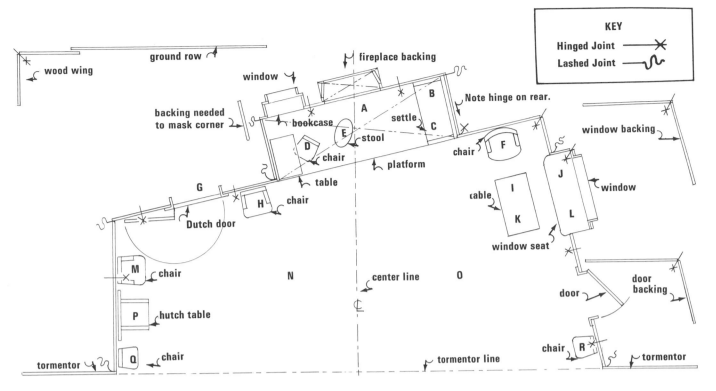

ground row

wood wing

window

fireplace backing

backing needed to mask corner

bookcase

settle

Note hinge on rear.

window backing

A

B

C

D

E

stool

chair

F

window

chair

platform

table

J

window backing

window

I

table

K

L

G

H

chair

Dutch door

window seat

M

chair

N

center line

O

door backing

P

hutch table

door

Q

chair

R

chair

tormentor

tormentor line

tormentor

Illus. 5. FLOOR PLAN FOR INTERIOR SET. This shows how the design in Illus. 3 and Illus. 4 could be rearranged to make it practical for a play. Test by arranging groups of model "actors." These can be merely scraps of wood or cardboard, but short, #6, flat-head screws are ideal as they are easy to handle. Place them, point up, on the plan and see how many ways you can find to group actors. All the seats and a few standing positions are lettered. Thus, you might try grouping two "actors" on F and J, three on M, G, and N, or four on A, C, D, and E. Remember that light furniture can be moved during the action to provide additional variety. For example, the hutch table, P, which now serves as a seat can be used as a table if it is moved away from the wall and has its top lowered. Again, someone can sit on chair D to write, turn it to face the settle, or get it out of the way by pushing it under the table.

The Nature of the Play. A set should tell the audience about the play as soon as the curtain goes up. Illus. 1 is religious. Illus. 2 is romantic. Illus. 3 is light and promises a comedy, and Illus. 6 is melodramatic.

Such differences in mood are vital. Spectators see the set before they see the play. If a set announces a play about real people and the play then turns out to be a fairy tale, the audience will be confused. If *Goldilocks and the Three Bears* were staged in Illus. 6, it would almost certainly fail. The setting would make the audience expect an entirely different kind of play.

Learn as much as you can about the play before you start to design. If it is about real people, make each set look like a real place. If the play is about imaginary characters, give your scenery impossible lines or colors to warn the spectators against taking the action seriously. When the play is cheerful, use light tones with touches of red or yellow. Gloomy or mysterious plays call for dark tones, thick draperies, and deep shadows like those in Illus. 6.

Economy of Construction

Scenery for school plays should ordinarily be inexpensive and simple if it is to be built at all—anything that wastes money or effort is poor design.

Even when you can afford elaborate sets, make certain that each feature is worth what it costs. Often fancy decorations are used where a plain wall would be better. There are sets where hours of hard work went into details that were covered by draperies or hidden by shadows. These examples do not mean that elaborate designs are wrong. Sometimes they repay all the trouble they take. Just be sure that yours justify it.

Learn as much as you can about the mechanics of scene construction. You will often find that a slight change in a design will turn a complicated job into an easy one. On the other hand, some feature which you hesitate to use because it seems difficult or costly may actually be easy—if you know how to make it.

Unfortunately, problems in building a model will

Illus. 6. PERSPECTIVE VIEW OF SET IN ILLUS. 5. This sketch shows the scene painted and lit for a mystery melodrama. The effect of gloom is heightened by closing the doors and drawing the curtains at the windows. If the set had been painted in pale tones, given lighter draperies, and brightly lit, it would look much like the shadow box in Illus. 3 and have the same cheery, wholesome atmosphere. Note that the side of the settle has been made narrower, so that it has less tendency to hide the face of an actor seated behind it.

not tell you much about the difficulty of building a full-sized set. Either a model or a set for marionettes could be made from the design in Illus. 2 without much trouble. However, constructing a full-scale version for live actors would be both laborious and costly.

On the other hand, making a detailed model from the designs in Illus. 5 and Illus. 6 would be a major task, but constructing a real set like this would be comparatively easy. If your group owns a collection of stock scenery, you may already have the walls, the ceiling, the platform, the large window, and the door in the side wall. There are not many special items, and only the Dutch door and the curved sides of the settle would give any trouble. In fact, an experienced stage carpenter could probably build a real set from scratch in less time than it would take him to make a detailed model for display purposes.

The working models that we are going to make as aids to design can be created quickly and easily. The important thing to remember is that neither the ease nor the difficulty that you find in building a model is a real guide to the effort required to construct an actual set. Whenever you design a set, always try to imagine the work involved. Then consider how you will feel if you learn later that you must do all the work yourself!

1. SCENERY AND THE STAGE

A working model is a tool, not a toy. It must fit the requirements of a real stage. If your model represents a set 30 feet wide, it will be useless for a play to be given on a church stage that is only 25 feet wide. On the other hand, a 25-foot set would be lost on a high school stage 40 feet wide.

Scenery

Sightlines. An important consideration is the relation of the set to the auditorium. When a set like the one in Illus. 7 is too small for the auditorium, the SIGHTLINES will reveal blind spots where large areas of the stage are invisible from some seats. Sightlines are equally important to show how wide to make the BACKINGS placed behind doors, windows and fireplaces. If they are too narrow, spectators can look through these openings and see parts of the backstage areas.

All types of design have similar practical requirements. It would be easy to design a dress that would be more becoming than anything women wear today. But a dress that is not in fashion will not sell, no matter how ugly the fashion happens to be.

When you plan model scenery, consider the needs of the BUILDING CREW, the director, and the actors. Such thinking is essential in designing things that *must* be practical, such as miniature radios or speedboats.

Equipment. The stage itself is merely the floor of a large room called the STAGE HOUSE. Study the parts in Illus. 8. No one knows how the TEASER and the TORMENTORS got their strange names, but they are extremely important. The teaser MASKS the FLIES. The tormentors mask the sides of the stage and serve as anchors for the edges of interior sets.

Each of the tormentors in Illus. 8 is made up of two flat pieces of scenery: the tormentor proper, which frames one side of the set; and a FLIPPER, which is a narrow piece that holds the tormentor erect and keeps people from seeing between it and the curtain. Some tormentors are much more elaborate and contain equipment for mounting stage lights.

Illus. 9 shows a plan of the stage. Here, the set is provided with RETURNS. These resemble tormentors without flippers and serve the same functions. However, they are parts of the set, whereas tormentors are permanent stage equipment like the curtain. Sets built for professional use normally include returns, which make them adaptable to stages of different widths when the play is on tour. Tormentors can rarely be moved more than a foot or two; returns permit larger adjustments.

Stage Geography. Although the floor of a stage is a bare rectangle, it has a geography of its own, which you must understand thoroughly before you can think about scenery intelligently.

The directions STAGE RIGHT, STAGE LEFT, UPSTAGE, and DOWNSTAGE are especially important. Unfortunately, you may find them confusing. Designers tend to think of a set from the front. When you do that, stage right is on your left.

Two other directions may also cause trouble. When we move an object ONSTAGE, we place it in a position where the audience can see it better. OFFSTAGE is the opposite of onstage. A door like the one down left in Illus. 9 is said to open offstage. Doors in sets normally open offstage. However, the Dutch door (which is like the one in Illus. 3) opens onstage. This was done because the upper part of the door makes a decorative feature when folded back.

These terms are also used to describe certain areas. Thus, the part of the stage within the set is an onstage area, whereas the parts hidden from the audience are offstage areas.

We also use ON STAGE (two words) and OFF STAGE.

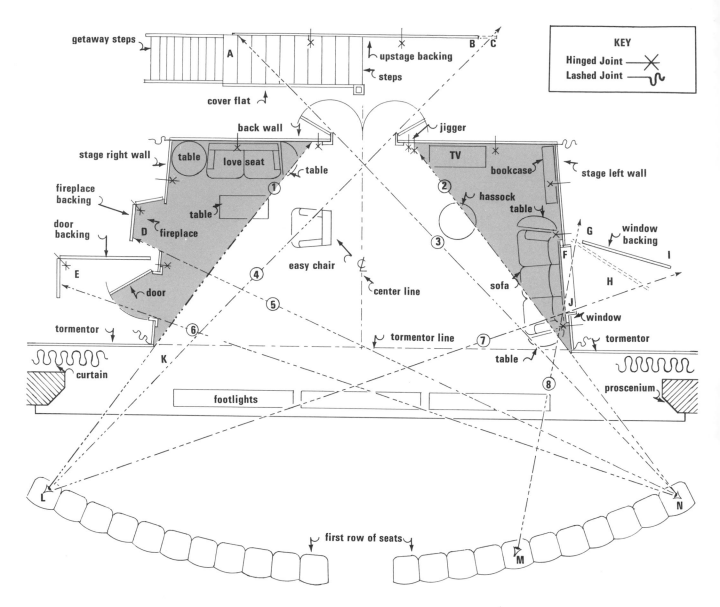

Illus. 7. PLAN OF SET WITH SIGHTLINES. Sightlines are drawn from key seats in the auditorium and tell us what parts of the stage can be seen by spectators in these seats. The seats on the ends of the first row are especially important. Thus, Sightline 1, drawn from Seat L past the edge of the set at Point K, shows that a person sitting at L will be unable to see anything which occurs in the shaded area. The other side of the stage behind Sightline 2 is hidden from an observer in Seat N. This situation always arises when the first row of seats is much wider than the set. Sightline 3 from Seat N strikes the backing at A and shows that the backing extends far enough in this direction. However, Sightline 4 from Seat L misses the end of the backing at Point B. Hence, the backing must be made wider so that it will reach Point C. Sightlines 5 and 6 from Seat N strike backings at Points D and E respectively. Therefore, no one in the audience can see actors or stage hands standing behind these backings. Sightline 7 from Seat L past Point J misses the backing at Point I, and Sightline 8 shows that a spectator in Seat M can see between Point F of the window and Point G of the backing. We can correct both faults either by using a larger backing or by turning the present backing into the position indicated by the dotted lines at H.

An actor walks on stage when he enters. A prop is taken off stage when an actor carries it with him as he exits. There is no distinction in speech between onstage (one word) and on stage (two words), but the difference in meaning should be understood. A simple test is to ask yourself whether you can insert the word "the." Thus, a prop shoved closer to a wall is "moved offstage." One carried completely off the set is "moved off (the) stage."

Pay special attention to the TORMENTOR LINE and the CENTER LINE—all dimensions are measured from them. Thus, we can locate the coffee table in Illus. 9 by saying that the corner marked *A* is 8 feet 5 inches (8'5") upstage of the tormentor line and 9 feet 6 inches (9'6") stage left of the center line. (Note that the symbol ' means "feet" and that " means "inches.")

The area downstage of the curtain line is the APRON. The offstage areas on either side of the set are known as the WINGS.

Axes

Every stage has two AXES. The TRANSVERSE AXIS runs across the stage parallel to the tormentor line. The DIRECT AXIS runs upstage-downstage parallel to the center line. (See Illus. 9.)

The set in Illus. 7 has its back wall on the transverse axis and is said to be PLACED PARALLEL. Such sets are normally a little wider in front than they are in back. This improves the sightlines and is never noticed by the audience. However, it keeps the side walls from being strictly on the direct axis.

Raked Sets. The scene in Illus. 5, Illus. 6, and Illus. 9 is arranged on a slant. All the walls are perpendicular to each other except the SHORT WALL on stage right. This plan results in a RAKED set and creates a second pair of axes known as the SET AXES (Illus. 9).

Illus. 10 shows how important it is to design your sets on axes. The general plan is the same as that in

Illus. 8. PERSPECTIVE VIEW OF STAGE HOUSE FROM WINGS. Study this in connection with the plan in Illus. 9. A gridiron or grid is essential in order to use drops and borders. Such scenery is said to be flown, and the space above the stage is called the flies. Unfortunately, many school stages lack grids. The teaser and the tormentors form the real frame of the stage picture.

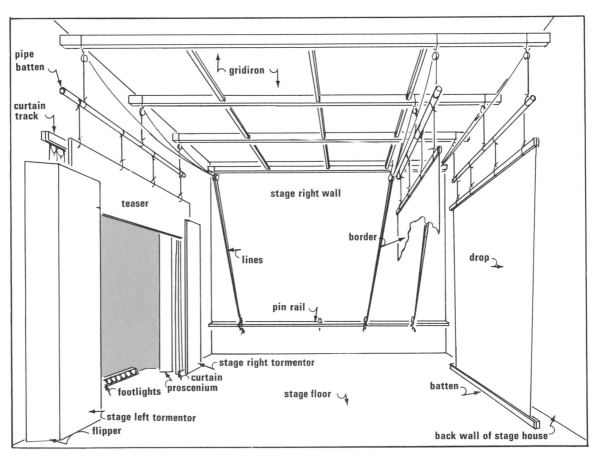

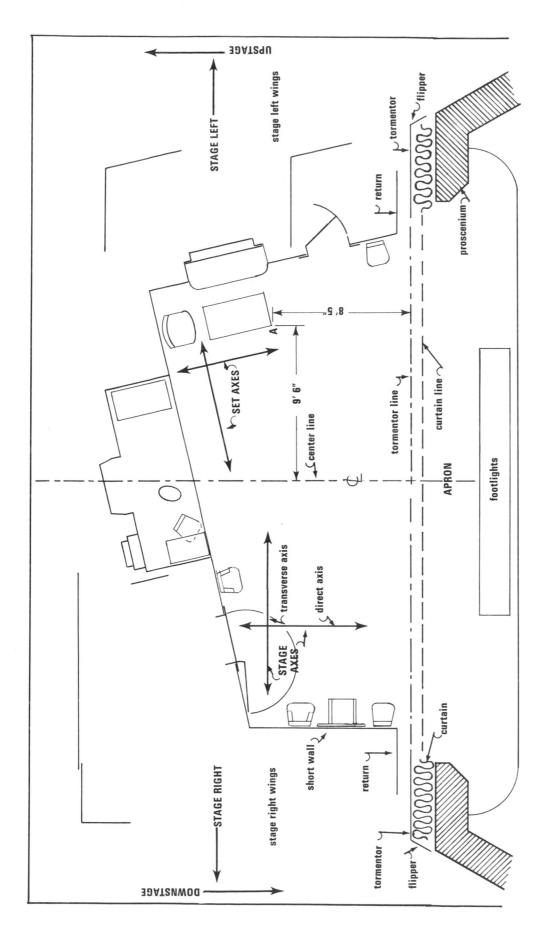

Illus. 9. STAGE GEOGRAPHY AND AXES. Stage right and stage left refer to the sides of an actor as he faces the audience. Old-fashioned stages sloped down towards the footlights. Hence, downstage means "towards the audience" and upstage means "away from the audience." The curtain touches the stage at the curtain line. The area between this and the footlights is the apron. If it is at least 3' deep, it can be used for short scenes while the main sets are being changed. The areas between the set and the side walls of the stage house are called the wings. There is no special name for the area behind the set.

A line drawn (or imagined) between the tormentors is called the tormentor line. The center line is at right angles to this and runs down the middle of the stage. These lines fix the stage axes. Anything parallel to the tormentor line is on the transverse axis. The back wall of the set in Illus. 7 is on this axis. Anything parallel to the center line is on the direct axis. The set outlined here (see Illus. 5) has its short wall on this direct axis. A scene placed on a slant is said to rake. When such a set has most of its walls at right angles to each other, it establishes a second pair of axes called the set axes.

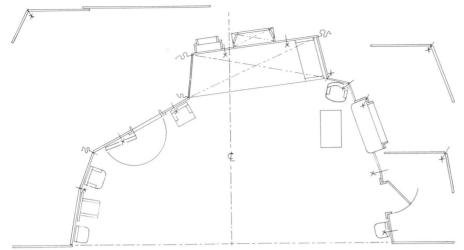

Illus. 10. IRREGULAR SET. This shows how Illus. 5 would look if the set axes were ignored. No real room has walls placed at random or furniture arranged without regard to the walls. As the parts are not organized on any definite scheme, this set is not really designed. Elaborate arrangements of steps and platforms are occasionally designed on a curve, but such cases are rare. Always begin by planning your sets on the stage axes, the set axes, or a combination of both.

Illus. 5. It could be used for the same play, and the sightlines are slightly better. However, it is unrealistic —rooms are not built like this—and its lack of order makes it a poor design.

Arranging Furniture. When a set is placed parallel, most of the furniture should be located on the stage axes (Illus. 7). However, if the side walls rake slightly, as they usually do, furniture near them should be located on the same angle as the walls. The bookcase and the down-left sofa follow this rule.

In a raked set like Illus. 5, most of the furniture should be parallel to the walls. When a short wall is on the direct axis, furniture near it is normally placed on the stage axes.

If we obey these rules strictly, the result may seem too formal. Thus, in Illus. 5 and Illus. 6, everything except the small stool is strictly ON AXIS. To achieve a more casual atmosphere place one or two chairs OFF AXIS, such as Chair D in the alcove of Illus. 5. The informal effect may not be noticeable in the plan, but it would be a strong element in an actual set.

A Model Stage House

You will need a model stage house for your sets (Illus. 11) in order to show them off better, and to make sure that your set will fit your real stage. It also provides an easy way to hang flown scenery.

There is no point in being fancy. Do not attach a floor to the walls. You will want to fold your model when it is not in use. You can make tormentors for your model stage, but it is more convenient to use returns. These can be simple rectangles of the same material as your set.

Illus. 11. A MODEL STAGE HOUSE. Make the walls of corrugated board cut from cartons used to pack large appliances. Join the corners by glueing 2″ strips of muslin over them. The floor can be a sheet of ½″ plywood or merely the top of an old table. No curtain is needed, but make a teaser out of carton board and hang it from strips of wood as shown.

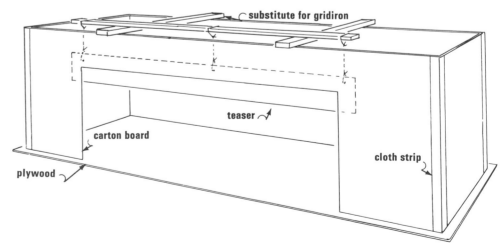

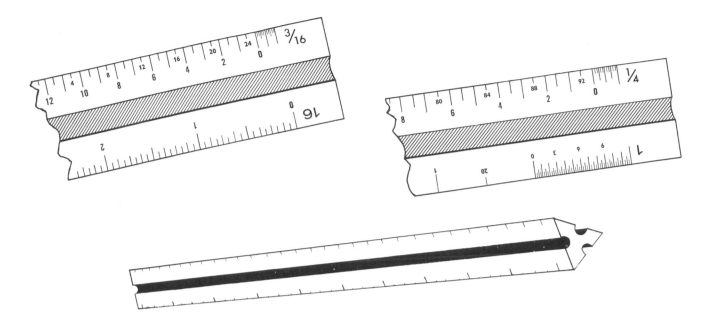

Illus. 12. ARCHITECT'S SCALE RULE. This makes it easy to build models to scale. In spite of its name, it is not a ruler. Use it only for measuring. If you rule lines with it, your pencil will soon spoil the fine markings. The type shown here carries ten different scales from $\frac{3}{32}''$=1' to 3"=1', and an ordinary footrule marked in sixteenths of an inch.

Scale

Your stage should be a SCALE MODEL of the actual stage in your auditorium. This means that every dimension should be in proportion to the measurements of your real stage.

The most convenient scale is 1"=1'. This is called a *one-inch scale*, and you use it when you make your model measure 1" for each 1' on the real stage. If your real PROSCENIUM, the part of the stage in front of the curtain, is 30' wide, your model proscenium should be 30" (2'6") wide.

You can make scale measurements with an ordinary ruler. Remember that $\frac{1}{2}''$ on the ruler equals 6" on the real stage, and $\frac{1}{4}''$ on the ruler equals 3" on the real stage. However, measuring is much easier when you use an *architect's scale rule* (Illus. 12). This is divided into scale feet and inches. The 1" scale shows half- and quarter-inches. The other scales on the rule are used just like the 1" scale, and you will find them handy later. For example, drawings of sets are normally made to a $\frac{1}{2}''$ scale. This means that each $\frac{1}{2}''$ on the drawing equals 1' on the stage.

As you can see from Illus. 12, a scale rule is divided in an unusual way. Have someone show you how to measure with it, or buy a student grade rule at a store selling artist's or draftsman's supplies and ask the clerk to explain its use. You will find this type of division extremely convenient.

2. TYPES OF SETS

Nearly all sets can be divided into a few standard types. There is no law against inventing new types or combining old ones. However, you will find it much easier to use the standard types at first, and the results will probably be better.

Drapery Sets

If your school is planning to produce a play and must use a drapery CYCLORAMA, or CYC, you may think there is no room for design. The cyc is draped cloth forming the walls of a set. However, there are many things you can do with a cyc to make it look like a real set. These will depend to some extent on the exact kind of cyc you have.

The best type is made up of cloth strips 9′ to 12′ wide. Strips like these can be hung to provide openings anywhere you want them. They can also be hung flat or in folds. Drapery hung in folds is said to have *fullness*. This is measured in percentages depending on the amount of extra cloth. Thus, if a 9′ drape is hung so that it is only 6′ wide, it has 3′ of material in the folds. This makes 50 per cent fullness, because 3′ is 50 per cent of 6′.

Most drapes have 50 per cent fullness. Anything more is usually wasted; anything less is apt to look skimpy. However, you may want to increase the fullness to create a rich effect. You may also want to hang your drapery flat to produce a night sky like that for the nativity scene in Illus. 1 (page 6).

Unfortunately, most school cycs have their fullness sewn into them. You cannot stretch them flat. You can add fullness by bunching the drape, but the result will never be as good as it would if you could handle the whole cloth to suit yourself.

The separate pieces of a high school cyc are usually too wide. Some have only two pieces of cloth in the back wall and one piece for each side wall. This lets actors enter at the center of the back and at the corners but nowhere else. As no real room has doors in the corners, such an arrangement makes any attempt at realism almost hopeless. If a cyc must be made up in wide pieces, there should be four pieces in the back wall and three in each side. That provides seven

Illus. 13. MAKESHIFT SET WITH DRAPERY WALLS. This is an example of how a few pieces of built scenery and a realistic arrangement of furniture can turn a drapery cyclorama into a fairly convincing interior. The mantelpiece is 1′ deep to make room for the fireplace without providing an opening behind it. The door frame and doors are also three-dimensional and need to be braced from the rear. Methods of constructing windows are shown in Illus. 14 and 15.

black cloth or carton board

rear view

Illus. 14. TYPE FOR NIGHT SCENE

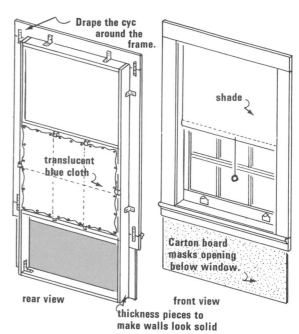

Illus. 15. TYPE

FOR DAY SCENE,

front and rear views

WINDOWS AND FRAMES FOR DRAPERY SETS

Drape the cyc around the frame.

translucent blue cloth

shade

Carton board masks opening below window.

rear view

front view

thickness pieces to make walls look solid

openings for doors, windows and fireplaces. You will probably never use all of them in one set, but it is convenient to have the choice.

Illus. 13 shows how to eke out a drape set with built pieces and props. The mantelpiece is merely placed in front of the drapery. A window in a night scene can be made like a picture frame and hung from the same support as the drape (Illus. 14). For a daytime scene, you may omit windows and pretend that they are in the missing wall of the set. If a window is used, it will need to be fairly elaborate because it must be lit from behind (Illus. 15). Windows for either day or night scenes should be covered by gauze curtains to keep the fraud from being too obvious.

A cyclorama of fairly light material with a lining is more satisfactory than an unlined cyclorama of heavy material. The face should be some pale tone, preferably light grey-blue. It has more life than light grey, and light tan is definitely drab. The lining should be navy blue.

A lined cyclorama actually gives you three choices. Use the pale side in most cases. The navy lining becomes blue when well lit; use it for special scenes like the Greek tent in Illus. 16. However, if the navy side is kept in darkness, it appears black. The night sky in the nativity scene in Illus. 1 (page 6) is a good example. A black lining would be no better for a night sky and could never be used for a scene like the Greek tent.

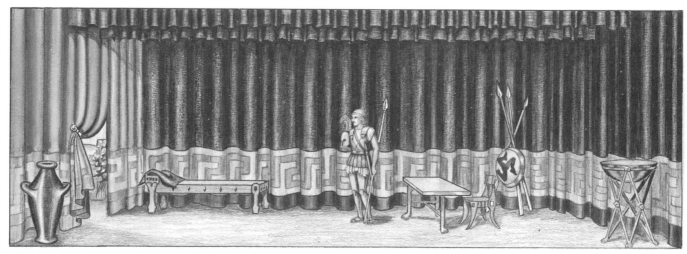

Illus. 16. TENT FOR GREEK WARRIOR. The design was painted on muslin and sewn lightly to navy-blue drapes. The sky backing seen through the opening is a large, flat piece of built scenery. The bushes are represented by another flat piece with a cut-out edge. Tying back the draperies at the door creates graceful curves that help the design. In most cases, you will find that cyclorama settings are improved by adding as many details as possible.

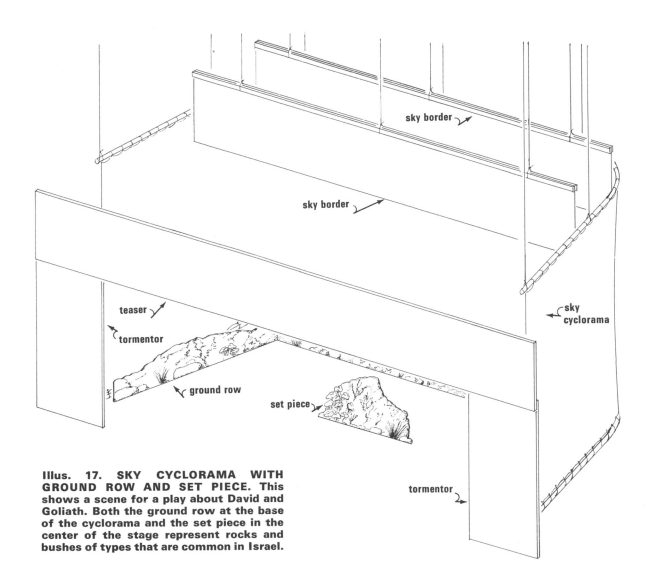

Illus. 17. SKY CYCLORAMA WITH GROUND ROW AND SET PIECE. This shows a scene for a play about David and Goliath. Both the ground row at the base of the cyclorama and the set piece in the center of the stage represent rocks and bushes of types that are common in Israel.

Symbolic Sets

Illus. 17 shows another type of cyclorama. This is a huge half-cylinder of cloth hung from above. Such a SKY CYCLORAMA masks the back and wings of the whole stage. If it is tall enough, it will mask the whole back wall of the stage house. In that case, the SKY BORDERS shown in the drawing can be omitted.

Although a sky cyclorama is primarily intended to create the illusion of a real sky in exterior scenes, it can also serve as a sort of generalized backing for sets that symbolize scenes instead of representing them realistically.

Set Pieces. Except for the cyc and the GROUND ROW needed to mask its lower edge, the whole setting in Illus. 17 consists of a single SET PIECE. This is a flat piece of scenery placed by itself somewhere in the playing space.

Few stages are equipped with sky cycloramas. However, as scenes like that in Illus. 17 make no serious attempts at realism, a drapery cyclorama could be substituted without much loss.

Partial Sets. The stable in Illus. 1 (page 6) carries the set-piece idea much further. It is three-dimensional and far more realistic. However, it does not represent a real stable—the front is open, and there are no doors. In night scenes like this, dark blue drapes are almost as effective as a sky cyclorama. That is true even for realistic exteriors.

The adobe chapel in Illus. 18 falls about halfway between a realistic set and an arbitrary one. The chapel is quite realistic up to a certain point. Anyone entering or leaving would use the door instead of merely walking through an imaginary wall as the actors would in Illus. 1. On the other hand, the chapel has no roof, and the characters would be

Illus. 18. PARTIAL SET SHOWING SPANISH MISSION CHAPEL. A sky cyclorama would improve this. However, as the setting is conventional, a drapery cyclorama can provide an adequate background. The illustration shows the drapes on the sides placed parallel to the tormentor line. This arrangement is not desirable, but it is fairly common on high school stages.

plainly visible as they cross a kind of no man's land between the wings and the actual set.

Few people know enough about Israel, Spanish missions, or Greek armor and furniture to design sets like those in Illus. 16 through Illus. 18 without doing research. You can usually find what you want in the Art and Geography Departments of the public library. If yours has a picture collection, you will find it a splendid research aid. For fairy-tale plays and other fantasies, the children's department is particularly valuable. Do not be afraid to ask librarians for assistance. Most of them will be only too happy to help you find what you want.

Unit Sets. Plays with many scenes, like those of Shakespeare, are often staged on an arrangement of platforms such as in Illus. 19. The larger platforms serve as miniature stages. When lit separately, they are used for scenes with only two or three characters. When a number of characters are present, the whole stage is lit and used.

Some unit sets require no changes except those that can be indicated by the lighting. However, many add other pieces of scenery, and a few require changes in the arrangement of the platforms. Anyone attempting to design a unit set needs a thorough knowledge of directing. Even then, you should work closely with the director. Otherwise, you are almost sure to have the director demand a high platform where you have put a low one, or a platform where your design indicates stairs.

Portal Sets. Illus. 20 shows another type of symbolic set suitable for plays of many scenes. The main element is a PORTAL, which is a kind of upstage proscenium. When curtains hung immediately in back of the portal are closed, the set provides a deep apron on which scenes can be played while the scenery behind the curtains is shifted.

Impressionistic Sets

At first sight, the shabby hotel room in Illus. 21 and Illus. 22 appears to belong in the same class as the nativity scene (Illus. 1) and the chapel (Illus. 18). However, it arouses an entirely different response. When you look at a real room, your vision has no sharp boundaries. It blurs at the edges. IMPRESSION-ISTIC scenery creates a similar effect by lighting the center of the set and letting it fade to darkness at the edges. While a spectator watches the action, he is never reminded that he is in a theatre by having his eye caught by a tormentor or one side of the proscenium. Furthermore, the sides of the set are masked by dark blue or black draperies or flats which obscure the actors before they enter and after they exit.

The whole point of an impressionistic set is its

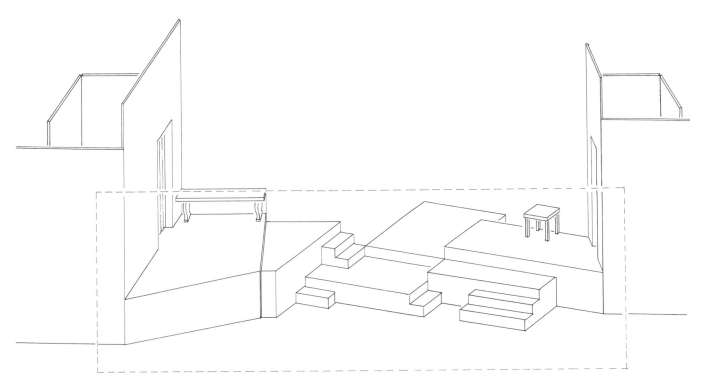

Illus. 19. UNIT SET FOR SHAKESPEARE'S "TWELFTH NIGHT". Scene changes are made by lighting different areas of the set. In this instance, the back wall of the stage house was plastered and painted a pale greyish blue, providing a useful and inexpensive substitute for a sky cyclorama. A drapery cyclorama can also be made to serve as a background for a unit set.

Illus. 20. PORTAL SET. This type of setting solves most masking problems and makes it easy to provide exteriors like the one shown here. As only the scenery on the inner stage is shifted, the amount needed for each set is comparatively small. A portal set is ideal for Shakespearean or classic plays.

Illus. 21. IMPRESSIONISTIC SET SHOWING ROOM IN CHEAP HOTEL. This is an excellent way to stage plays with many sets. If all the scenes are laid in the same building, such as a hospital or an apartment house, you can use the same walls and doors for every set. Different arrangements and props keep the scenes from seeming too much alike. Another advantage is that the scenery can be shifted in much less time than you would need for sets that occupied the whole stage.

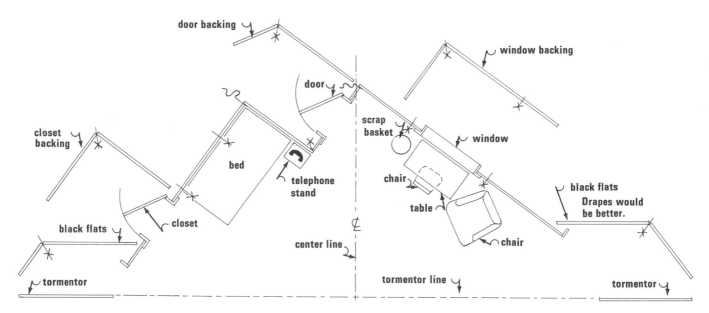

Illus. 22. FLOOR PLAN OF SET IN ILLUS. 21. The sides of impressionistic sets must be masked. Dark drapes running on tracks hung from the gridiron are ideal. If no grid is available, you can use flat pieces of scenery painted black instead of the drapes.

realism. The actors behave like real people, and nothing should look faked.

Drops, Borders, and Wings

Musicals often require a number of different scenes. In most cases, the only practical way to handle these is by using a backdrop and masking the flies with borders and WINGS (Illus. 23). Do not confuse the wings, which are areas on the sides of the stage, with wings, which are pieces of scenery placed on the sides of the playing space.

Most sets of this nature also need one or more ground rows to mask the unrealistic line where the drop meets the stage. Wings and ground rows are MASKING PIECES.

All of these pieces are normally flat. Drops and borders are kept flat by gravity. Wings and ground rows are stiffened with wooden frames so that they can stand alone. This is also true of set pieces.

Wings, ground rows, and set pieces usually have irregular edges and are grouped together under the term CUTOUTS. They can be distinguished by their positions. Wings are used at the sides of the stage,

Illus. 23. DROPS, BORDERS, AND WINGS. This is an appropriate set for a musical or a ballet. Drops and borders require a grid and some sort of rigging system to raise and lower them. The set shown uses two ground rows. The yew trees are painted on the drop. However, if your stage has a sky-blue back wall, you could make the trees as set pieces and put them behind the ground rows. (See Illus. 24 for a hint on painted perspective.)

ground rows at the rear, and set pieces in the playing space. Most wings are tall and narrow; ground rows are broad but not high; set pieces tend to be about as high as they are wide. Designers would often prefer to do without them but are forced to use them because there is something to hide. Set pieces, on the other hand, are essentially symbols. They provide a way

of saying, "This is a rock," or "This is a fountain in the village square." A set piece rarely serves any other purpose—in fact, it may even be a nuisance because it hides actors who walk behind it.

The caption for Illus. 24 explains a point that anyone attempting to paint perspective on scenery must understand.

Illus. 24. PERSPECTIVE SET FOR OLD-FASHIONED MELODRAMA. Musicals and old-fashioned melodramas sometimes use scenery painted in perspective. If you understand perspective and want to use it on scenery, you will have trouble unless you learn one simple trick. The ordinary rules apply to the backdrop. But, if you apply them to the wings, you will get the unsatisfactory effect shown on the stage-right wings in the sketch. The correct procedure is illustrated on stage left.

Everything above the horizon follows the normal rules, so that horizontal lines running into the stage picture slant downward to their vanishing points. Theoretically, similar lines below the horizon should slant up, as they do on stage right. This would place the ground lines at a series of angles instead of making them continuous. We can avoid that awkward effect by keeping these lines parallel to the floor, as on stage left. The bases of the columns in Illus. 23 were drawn in this way.

Illus. 25. EXTERIOR SET. You cannot expect a daytime exterior to be much more realistic than this. The steps, both large tree trunks, and some of the rocks are three-dimensional. But everything else will show up as merely paint on flat canvas. Exteriors based on axes are likely to seem formal and unrealistic. This one was planned on a curve.

Exteriors

Exterior scenes laid at night can be quite convincing, but those laid in daytime are rarely successful, mostly because of the masking problem. Unless a sky cyclorama is available, the designer must introduce borders to conceal the flies and find some way to mask the wings on both sides (Illus. 25).

Borders in exterior scenes are usually painted to represent foliage, and their lower edges are cut away. Only the part above the deepest cut serves as a mask (see dotted lines in Illus. 26 and Illus. 27). Everything below this level merely makes a conventional gesture toward realism. Study Illus. 28 and the vertical sightlines in Illus. 29.

Professional borders are usually cut out in elaborate patterns and will not keep their shape unless the holes are backed with coarse net (Illus. 26). The fancy part of the border must be hung low so that the upper part will mask. Unfortunately, that brings the bottom down far enough to catch the eyes of the audience and call attention to its lack of reality.

The conventional borders in Illus. 25 and 27 are both less costly and easier to construct. However, as the "fringes" do not hang down very far, they attract little or no notice. This simple type of border is just as convincing as the elaborate variety in Illus. 2 and Illus. 26.

Although not much can be done to improve exterior borders, something can be done about the wings. Thus, the wall of the chapel in Illus. 25 is set at an angle so that it masks one whole side. Also, the realism of the wall itself is increased by setting the door back to show the THICKNESS of the wall. In this case, the stage-left side had to be masked by WOOD WINGS, which is much less satisfactory.

Whenever a scene permits, try to find realistic masking pieces for both sides. Suppose a scene is laid in the dooryard of a farmhouse. The house will mask one side, but what about the other? Wood wings would be unrealistic. Even if they were not flat cutouts, few dooryards have a solid wall of trees so close to the house. You can solve this by putting the house on one side and a barn or stable on the other. If the barn is also set at an angle, it will provide all the masking you need, and the effect will be much more convincing than wood wings could possibly be.

Interiors

Most interiors are staged in BOX SETS. The reason for the name is obvious when the set is merely a large canvas box (Illus. 30). However, although the one in Illus. 6 (page 10) is far from boxlike, it is still called a box set.

We can rarely design a box set so that spectators on the extreme ends of the first row can see the entire stage. Even if the set in Illus. 7 (page 12)

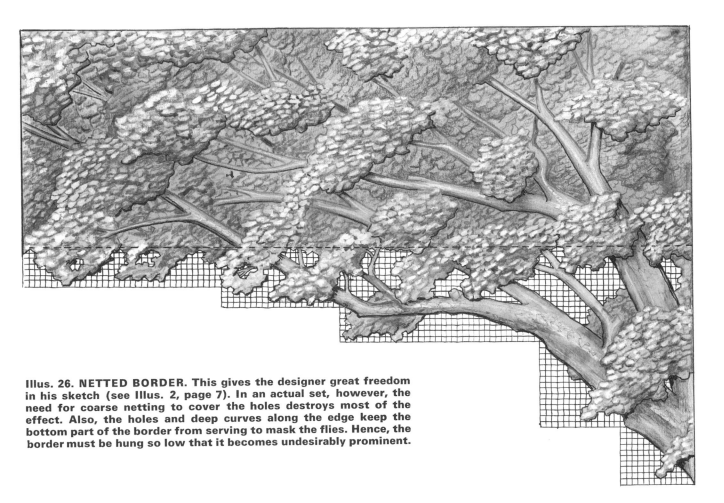

Illus. 26. NETTED BORDER. This gives the designer great freedom in his sketch (see Illus. 2, page 7). In an actual set, however, the need for coarse netting to cover the holes destroys most of the effect. Also, the holes and deep curves along the edge keep the bottom part of the border from serving to mask the flies. Hence, the border must be hung so low that it becomes undesirably prominent.

Illus. 27. BORDER RECOMMENDED FOR AMATEURS. This type seems crude in a sketch, but it needs no netting. As almost the whole border provides masking, it may be hung at teaser height where it will attract little attention. Paint the back of the lower edge as well as the front. This will stiffen the leaves and reduce their tendency to curl. Parts that overhang like those at C and D will curl badly. Make every line cut back like those at A and B.

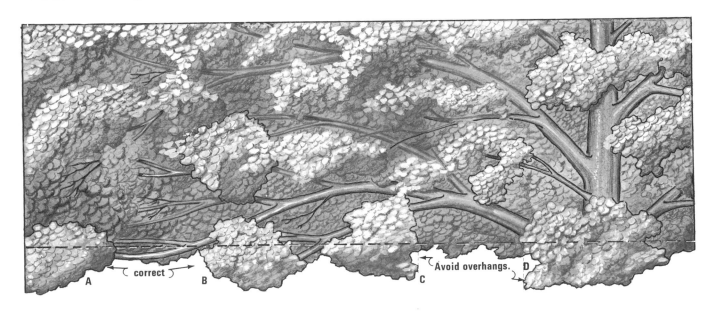

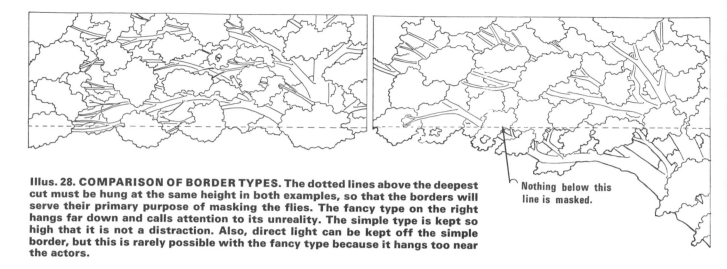

Illus. 28. COMPARISON OF BORDER TYPES. The dotted lines above the deepest cut must be hung at the same height in both examples, so that the borders will serve their primary purpose of masking the flies. The fancy type on the right hangs far down and calls attention to its unreality. The simple type is kept so high that it is not a distraction. Also, direct light can be kept off the simple border, but this is rarely possible with the fancy type because it hangs too near the actors.

Nothing below this line is masked.

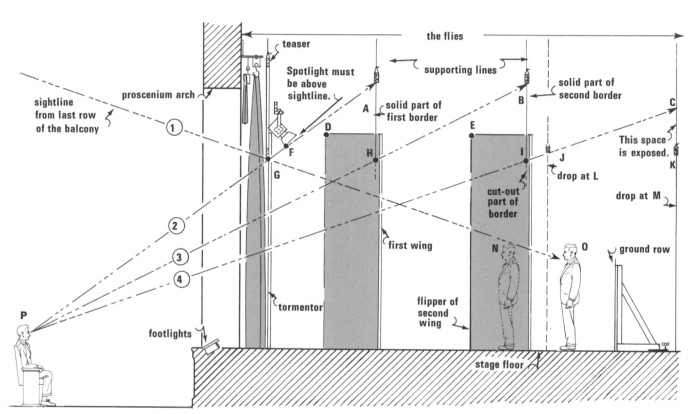

Illus. 29. VERTICAL SIGHTLINES FOR EXTERIORS. The lower edge of the teaser is the key (Point G). Sightline 2 from a spectator in the first row (Point P) and passing Point G must be below the lights behind the teaser (Point F) and also below the top of the first border (Point A). Sightline 3 then passes just under the deepest cut of this border (Point H) and must strike the second border below Point B. Sightline 4 passes beneath the deepest cut of this border (Point I). It should then strike the drop at Point K. However, in the drawing it passes over the drop at Point C. We can correct this by: (1) using a higher drop; (2) raising the drop and masking its lower edge with a ground row; (3) bringing the drop downstage from its present position at M to Position L. Sightline 4 will then strike it at Point J; (4) adding a third border. Which method is best will depend on the set and the equipment of your stage. The wings in the drawing are masked by the borders. However, their flippers are so low that spectators can see over them (D and E). They should be high enough to bring their tops level with the tops of the borders. If the auditorium has a balcony, a spectator in the last row must be able to look under the teaser (Point G) and see the face of an actor standing far upstage in Position O. When this is not possible, we must either raise the teaser—which will change Sightlines 2, 3, and 4—or we must keep actors from moving further upstage than Position N. Exteriors with high platforms upstage (Illus. 25) create major sightline problems in theatres with balconies. If your auditorium has a balcony, work out the sightlines before designing the set. Otherwise, you may have to make an entirely different design—or worse still, discover at the first dress rehearsal that actors on the platforms cannot be seen by spectators seated in the balcony.

Illus. 30. BOX SET. This is similar to the set in Illus. 7 (page 12) but is 30′ wide instead of only 25′. I have used the extra room to substitute a sofa for the love seat on stage right and a bench for the hassock on stage left. I have also added chairs on either side of the television set to avoid blank spots and provide additional places to sit.

were 4′ wider, there would still be blind areas in the upstage corners that would be hidden from a few spectators. Raked sets like that in Illus. 6 have better sightlines. But even with these, it is difficult to avoid blind areas entirely.

Try to fill the blind areas with tables and bookcases and to avoid using them for chairs and sofas. However, do not sacrifice desirable features for the sake of a few spectators. In Illus. 6, for example, the window seat is hidden from a small part of the audience. In spite of this, it adds greatly to the set.

A director should not place a character there if he has an important part in a major scene, but it can be used for minor characters or even for major characters in minor scenes where they are not part of the main action. Furthermore, an actor on either the window seat or the settle should sit near the edge and lean forward whenever he is speaking.

Vertical sightlines rarely cause trouble with interiors unless the auditorium has a balcony. Illus. 31 shows the chief points to watch.

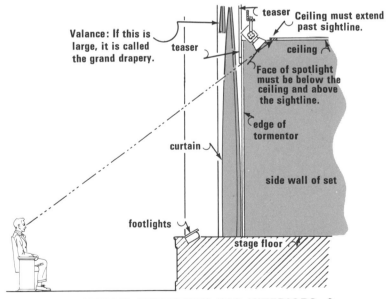

Illus. 31. VERTICAL SIGHTLINES FOR INTERIORS. A single sightline is enough to tell us whether or not a spectator in the first row can see either the lights in back of the teaser or the space downstage of the ceiling. When there is a balcony, we have problems corresponding to the ones in Illus. 29.

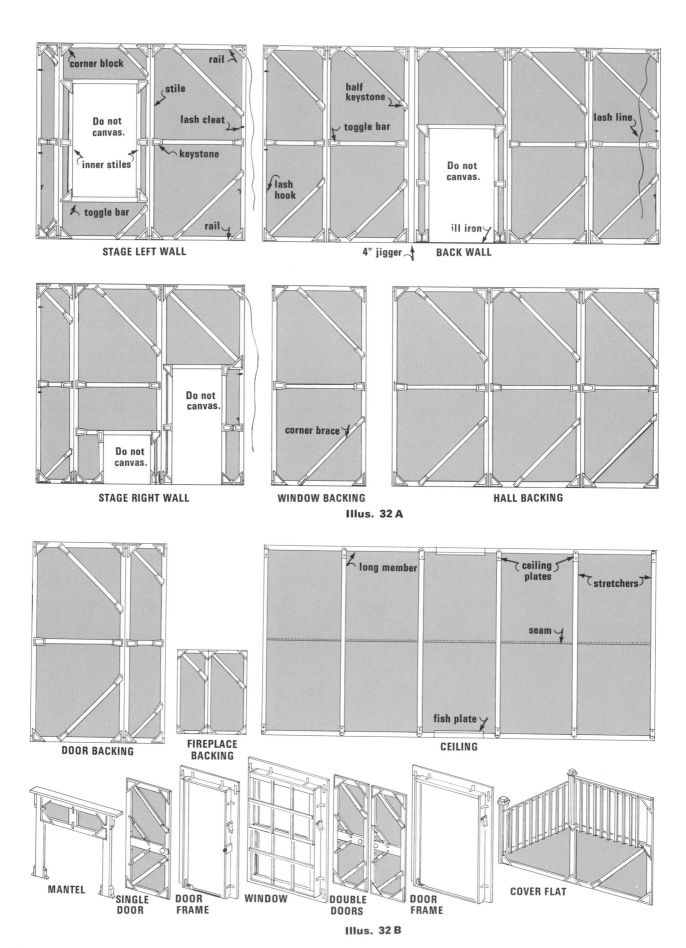

STAGE LEFT WALL

corner block

rail

stile

lash cleat

Do not canvas.

keystone

inner stiles

toggle bar

rail

half keystone

toggle bar

lash line

Do not canvas.

lash hook

ill iron

4" jigger

BACK WALL

STAGE RIGHT WALL

Do not canvas.

Do not canvas.

WINDOW BACKING

corner brace

HALL BACKING

Illus. 32 A

DOOR BACKING

FIREPLACE BACKING

long member

ceiling plates

stretchers

seam

fish plate

CEILING

MANTEL

SINGLE DOOR

DOOR FRAME

WINDOW

DOUBLE DOORS

DOOR FRAME

COVER FLAT

Illus. 32 B

28

3. THE NATURE OF SCENERY

The average spectator thinks of a set as being all one piece, which is, in fact, what we want him to think. Actually, however, each set is made up of many pieces called SCENE UNITS. Illus. 32 through 34 show the thirty-one units that make up the small living-room set in Illus. 7 (page 12).

Flats

The basic wall unit is the FLAT (Illus. 32). The ideal height for a flat is 12′. Anything shorter makes the set look crushed down. Taller flats require heavier lumber and two TOGGLE BARS instead of one. They are also hard for inexperienced stagehands to manage. With 12′ flats, the teaser will be about 10′ 6″ above the stage. This is excellent when the auditorium has no balcony. However, if there is a balcony, the teaser must be raised. That calls for flats that are 14′ or even higher.

Flats vary in width from 1′ to 5′ 9″. The maximum is fixed by the fact that a flat more than 5′ 9″ cannot be covered with a single piece of canvas. Also, this is the widest flat that one stagehand can manage easily. When you need a flat less than 1′ wide, use a plain board instead.

Flats are marvels of engineering (Illus. 32). Although they are only a trifle over 1″ thick, they are practically indestructible. I have staged 72 full-length plays, many with two or more scenes. My stagehands rarely had much experience. Nevertheless, in all that time, I never had a flat warp or get out of square—and only a single piece of wood in one flat was ever broken. However, *unless the flats are properly built of the right materials, they will give endless trouble and will soon fall to pieces.*

Books. Most walls are over 5′ 9″ wide. They are made by hinging two or more flats together (Illus. 35) into a BOOK. This leaves an unsightly crack which must be covered by narrow bands of canvas called STRIPPERS (Illus. 36).

Jiggers. When a book contains more than two flats, they must be arranged so that they can be folded. Folding is impossible if a three-fold book has all three flats the same size, or if the smallest flat is in the middle. However, we can get around the difficulty by inserting a JIGGER between two of the flats (Illus. 37 and Illus. 38). A jigger is simply a strip of wood the height of the flats. The one shown is 3″ wide. Cover it with a 7″ stripper to hide the cracks on both sides.

Jiggers make possible walls containing five flats or even more. Illus. 7 (page 12) and Illus. 30 (page 27) show where this has been managed with one 4″ jigger. However, you may occasionally need two. In that case, the second jigger must be 6″ wide.

Hinging Plans. Arranging flats in books is an important part of the designer's work. Most of the plans show the locations of the hinges. Study these carefully. The problems involved may look easy when you see the solutions worked out. Actually, nine out of ten are routine—but the tenth can be extremely difficult.

If we let two books come together in a wall, there would be no way to hide the crack between them. Each wall must consist of a single book. Of course, if two short walls meet at a corner, they can both be parts of one book. The up-left corner of the set in Illus. 5 (page 9) shows a book of three flats. One joint is hinged on the face and covered with a

Illus. 32. (Opposite) WALL AND CEILING UNITS FOR SMALL SET IN ILLUS. 7 (page 12). This shows the backs of thirteen plain flats, a window flat, one flat for a double door, one for a single door, and one for a fireplace. These, with the jigger, are grouped into five books. Three books make up the main set. The other two, and the single flat, serve as backings. The set also includes two door frames with doors, a window, a mantelpiece, a fireplace backing, a ceiling, and a cover flat to hide the exposed sides of the steps and the platform, both of which are shown here. This makes thirty-two units all told.

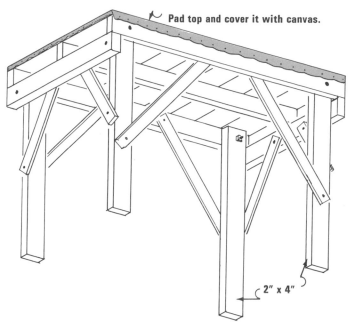

Illus. 33. PLATFORM FOR SET IN ILLUS. 7 (page 12). In order to reveal the construction of these units, I have drawn them from below and used a larger scale than I did for the units in Illus. 32. A platform over 7' long will need an extra set of legs in the middle. Platform heights can be adjusted by substituting longer or shorter legs.

Pad top and cover it with canvas.

2" x 4"

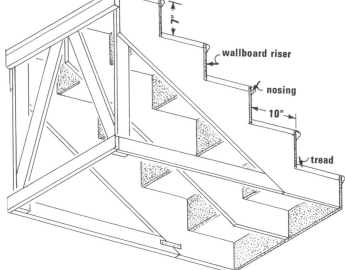

7"

wallboard riser

nosing

10"

tread

Illus. 34. STEPS FOR SET IN ILLUS. 7 (page 12). Professional scene builders use a different type of platform which supports the top of the steps. However, the platform shown in Illus. 33 is better for amateur use. This requires steps which will stand alone. The dimensions given for the treads and risers create a steep stair, but this is desirable in scene design. Make the risers of wallboard and fasten nosings of moulding to the edges of the threads with 8-penny finishing nails.

stripper. The other is hinged on the back without a stripper.

Joining Books. When two books meet at a corner, they are normally held together by LASHING (Illus. 39). Lashing always leaves a slight crack. However, this will be invisible if the flat running across stage overlaps the one running up- and down-stage.

When a play needs only one set, you can save a little trouble by nailing books together instead of lashing them. Flats 3 and 4 in Illus. 39 are joined in this way.

Jogs. A JOG is a break in a wall made by a single flat like Flat 2 in Illus. 39 or even by a single board like the one shown between Flats 5 and 6. Jogs have several uses. When a wall is too long to be easily handled as a unit, introducing a jog allows breaking it up into two books. Jogs also stiffen the set—long walls tend to wobble and should be braced. Large jogs increase the amount of wall space and also make the floor plan more interesting than a simple rectangle. Most of the sets in this book use at least one jog.

Other Two-Dimensional Units

A ceiling is essentially a large flat (Illus. 32B). A drop has one BATTEN at the top and another at the bottom to keep it rigid (Illus. 8, page 13). The top should be about 2' wider than the bottom so that the sides taper. If they are made vertical, the lower corners of the drop will develop unsightly wrinkles.

Borders are like drops except that they have no bottom batten (Illus. 2, 25, 26, 27 and 28).

Cutouts. Ground rows, wings, and set pieces usually have irregular edges, and many of them are pierced with irregular or random holes (Illus. 40 and Illus. 41). If these are designed only for artistic effect without practical consideration, they can give the building crew a great deal of unnecessary trouble. To the eye, the set piece in Illus. 40 is not noticeably different from the one in Illus. 41. Nevertheless, the one in Illus. 40 involves a major construction job, whereas the one in Illus. 41 can be put together in short order.

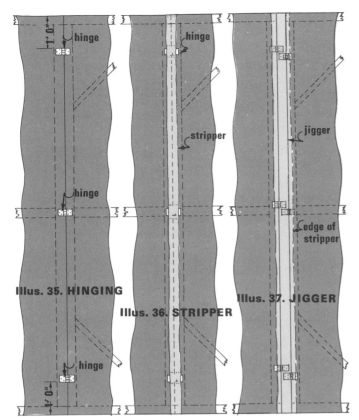

Illus. 35. HINGING

Illus. 36. STRIPPER

Illus. 37. JIGGER

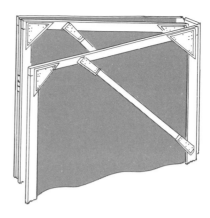

Illus. 38. WHY A JIGGER MAY BE NEEDED. Illus. 35 shows where hinges are located. In Illus. 36, the crack has been covered with a 4″ stripper held in place with paste and tacks. Strippers that are too wide will work loose. Hence, they should not cover the ends of the hinges. This does no harm, as paint will hide them. Illus. 37 shows how a narrow board called a jigger is hinged between two flats to give room so that a book like the one above can be folded.

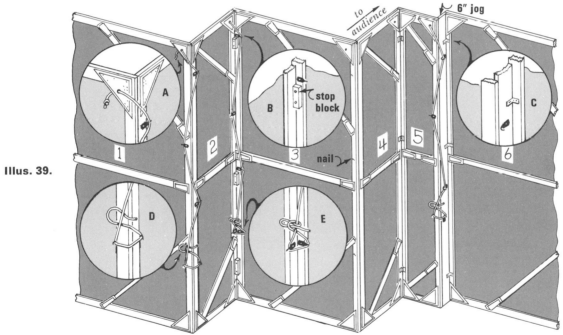

Illus. 39.

Illus. 39. METHODS OF JOINING FLATS AT CORNERS. Flat 1 has been lashed to the upstage edge of Flat 2. The lash line of ¼″ sash cord is passed through a hole in the corner block and knotted (Inset A). It is then lashed around lash cleats and finally tied off around lash hooks (Inset D). This is the normal method of joining flats at corners. The line can also be tied off around lash cleats (Inset E), but the knot used is more elaborate. Flat 2 meets Flat 3 in a reverse corner. In this case, stop blocks are needed (Inset B). Without these, the line would pull the corner apart instead of holding it together. Flats 4 and 5 also make a reverse corner. However, these are joined with hinges. The stage left wall of the alcove in Illus. 5 (page 9) has been hinged in this way. Flat 3 is

nailed to Flat 4 with three 8-penny finishing nails driven at a downward angle. The heads project ¼″ so that the nails can be drawn easily. Nailing is convenient on one-set shows. However, it is a nuisance when scenes must be shifted, because a stagehand must climb a ladder to draw the top nail. When a narrow jog is to be lashed, lash hooks must be substituted for lash cleats. A jog can be hinged to the rear of another flat, but corner irons that hold it rigidly in place are better (Inset C). Note that in all these cases the cross-stage flat overlaps the one which runs up-and-down stage. There is always a narrow crack where two flats join. Spectators can see through this if the flats overlap in the other direction.

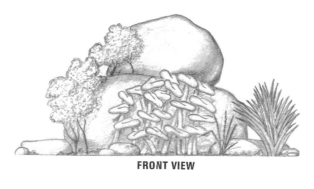

FRONT VIEW

FRONT VIEW

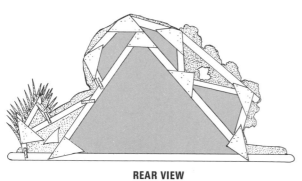

REAR VIEW

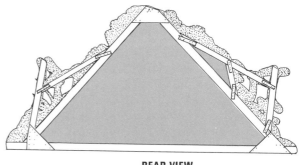

REAR VIEW

Illus. 40. POORLY DESIGNED CUTOUT. This is the set piece used in Illus. 17 (page 19). The plant with broad fleshy leaves is like a cactus and grows in Israel. The rear view shows that the design calls for a complex construction which will be hard to build, heavy, and expensive.

Illus. 41. WELL DESIGNED CUTOUT. The front view here looks almost like that in Illus. 40, but the rear views are entirely different. This is framed simply with a maximum of canvas and minimum of lumber and construction.

The structural design of a cutout depends on three factors. The irregular edge must be cut from some thin, light, but stiff material such as wallboard or carton board. If this extends past the main frame more than about 6″, it might break off. Even the lightest edging material is heavier than canvas, so it is desirable to use as little of it as possible. Finally, the frame will not be rigid unless it is designed as a series of triangles. To prove this, nail strips of wood together to make a figure with four or five sides. Then see how easily it can be twisted out of shape.

Cover Flats. The scene units used for platforms and steps are open at the sides (Illus. 33 and Illus. 34), and must be masked in some way. When there are no railings, this can be done by nailing wallboard or carton board over the openings. Interior stairways, however, usually have railings. These are provided by COVER FLATS as shown in Illus. 32B. The exterior platforms in Illus. 20 (page 21) are

masked by cutouts. If these are attached to the platforms, they are called cover flats; if they stand alone, they are set pieces. In either case, the construction is the same.

Moulding. The use of moulding can do wonders to enhance the appearance of an interior set. In Illus. 13 (page 17), the door, the door frame, and the fireplace are all decorated with moulding. The lip on the window sill is also moulding. The picture frame on the left is made of flat boards with a strip of moulding around the edges. The NOSING on the steps in Illus. 34 is moulding held in place with 8-penny finishing nails.

If you use a separate type of moulding for each purpose, it can be expensive. Fortunately, small differences cannot be noticed by the audience. The type in Illus. 42 can be used for everything from cornices to chair rails.

This advantage is partly offset by the fact that

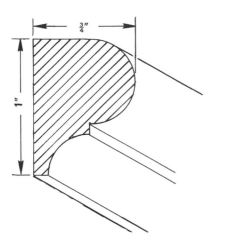

Illus. 42. MOULDING. The type shown here can be used for every stage purpose from picture frames to the nosing on steps.

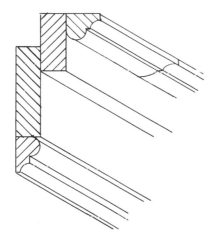

Illus. 43. CORNICE. Even small scraps can be used if you nail them to a base made from narrow, white-pine boards.

Illus. 44. NAILING PANELS. These are rigid and easy to build. They can be used to decorate either doors or walls (see Illus. 6, page 10).

few lumber yards stock the type in Illus. 42. You may need to have a special cutter made, which is fairly expensive. However, once you have it, you can use moulding lavishly at little cost. Even small scraps can be used over and over again. Thus, the cornice in Illus. 43 was constructed by attaching random lengths of moulding to the boards with 4-penny finishing nails. When this was done, the ends of the pieces were mitered so that they overlap. Otherwise, the crack would be visible.

The method of making panels is shown in Illus. 44. Panels are used to decorate the doors in Illus. 13 (page 17). The doors were made like small flats with extra corner braces (see the doors in Illus. 32B). The panels were then nailed to the braces.

Three-Dimensional Units

No scenery is really solid, and making it look solid means extra work. Even platforms and steps require cover flats.

Thickness. Scenery is more convincing when the thickness of the walls is shown. Compare the "picture frame" window in Illus. 14 (page 18) with the more realistic window in Illus. 15. The door and the little belfry of the mission in Illus. 18 (page 20) have special THICKNESS PIECES to emphasize the solidity of the walls. When the edge of a wall shows, a thickness piece is essential. These small units are harder to build than the walls themselves, but they make the difference between an impressive set and a flimsy one. Time and money devoted to thickness pieces are usually well spent.

Irregular Forms. Rocks, tree trunks, and other irregular shapes that need not bear weight are easy to make. Simply build a light framework, mould 2″ chicken wire over it and cover this with canvas (Illus. 45).

Practical Units. Most scenery is for appearance only and is not designed to actually work—windows cannot be opened, and trees cannot be climbed. However, when a unit must work it is said to be PRACTICAL.

Special Effects. These can take almost any form such as doors with panels that can be knocked in so that someone outside can reach through the hole and turn the lock, and bottles that break when struck by imaginary bullets. I once staged an elaborate old-fashioned melodrama in which a night club burned down, the hero fell through the floor, and one wall collapsed on the villain. With so many possibilities, there can be no rules. The designer must depend on his ingenuity.

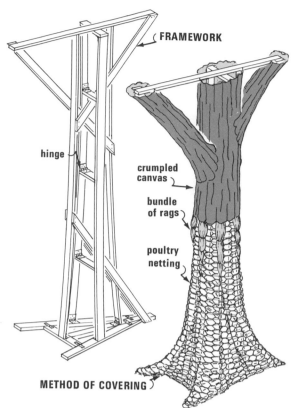

FRAMEWORK

hinge

crumpled
canvas

bundle
of rags

poultry
netting

METHOD OF COVERING

Illus. 45. TRUNK FOR TREE. This type is inexpensive and much easier to build than it may seem at first glance. It is light enough to be shifted by a single stagehand.

Weight-Bearing Units. Almost the only weight-bearing units worth considering for school plays are steps and platforms (Illus. 33 and 34, page 30). These add interest to the design of a set. They also permit a director to provide both variety and drama by grouping his actors on different levels. Always include steps and platforms in sets whenever the nature of the scene permits it.

Platforms are easy to build. If you have somewhere to store them, you can have a stock set which may be used for almost any play, and the cost-per-use becomes very small.

Steps are less flexible. You may need a set with three steps for one set and five steps for another. You may also need to vary the widths. As there is no way to make steps adjustable, you must build new ones to fit each situation. Nevertheless, you can often use existing steps in new scenes.

Scene Construction

Although I lack space here to explain the details of full-scale scene construction, several excellent books on the subject are available. Learn all you can from them. You will need this knowledge to design effective scenery. Furthermore, it will help you to form the habit of thinking in practical terms. Too many designers think only of appearances. They design things that are unnecessarily difficult or expensive to build. They sacrifice important practical advantages to minor artistic effects. I could cite hundreds of examples ranging from the push buttons on spray cans to the arrangement of bookshelves in libraries. You can almost certainly find many for yourself.

If you do much work on a school stage, compile a list of all the ways that the architect could have made practical improvements *without either increasing the cost or harming the appearance of the auditorium.* Remember not to create designs that show no consideration for either those who will make them or those who will use them.

4. MODEL SCENERY

Illus. 46 shows the layout for a display model of the set in Illus. 30. However, the effect is quite different because the walls have been redecorated and a new style of furniture has been introduced. Note the use of moulding to make wall panels and also how much the use of diagonals changes the appearance of the set. Illus. 47 represents the completed model in a slightly more elaborate version.

Display models are made to show people how the set will look. The simple type with most of the details painted on the walls can be made in less time than a sketch and requires no knowledge of perspective. However, such a model does not help the designer, because he must plan the set before he can make the model.

Experienced designers work out their sets with the aid of rough sketches. Students will make better progress if they use a working model. The type in Illus. 48 through Illus. 50 can be built quickly out of carton board. It forces you to think in terms of actual construction. For example, if you hinge a 3' model flat between two 5' 9" flats, the model book cannot be folded. It is much better to learn such things from the model than to have them forced on your attention after the real scenery is hinged, and perhaps painted.

Best of all, such a model lets you experiment with the least possible effort. If you are not satisfied with one version of a set, you can rearrange the parts in a matter of minutes—even if you need to cut out a few more flats.

Walls

The walls of your working model will consist of flats hinged in books. Cut each flat from carton board. The flats must be to scale, that is, if you are using a scale of $1'' = 1'$, a flat 12' high and 5' 9" wide will measure $12'' \times 5\frac{3}{4}''$.

Layout. This must be done accurately. If the edges of the flats are ragged or crooked, they will not hinge properly and you may have trouble making them stand erect. Although the procedure described in Illus. 48 is satisfactory, layout is much easier if you use a *drawing board*, a *T square* and a *triangle*. As these are basic tools for advanced design, you should start learning to handle them as soon as possible.

Cutting. You can cut carton board with heavy shears. However, it is hard on the shears, and the result will be rough. A better procedure is to use a *metal straightedge* and a sharp knife. Do *not* cut along the edge of a T square. You will nick it no matter how careful you try to be. X-acto knives are good for cutting out flats. Art stores also sell knives designed especially for making straight cuts in thin materials. Do your work on a *cutting board*, or you will scar your table. A sheet of $\frac{1}{8}''$ hardboard makes an ideal cutting board. Place the straightedge along one line of the layout and make the cut as though you were ruling a line with a pencil.

As you cut out each flat, write its width on the back with a marking pen, so you will not have to measure the flat each time you pick it up.

Mark doors and windows on the flats but do not cut them out. Real flats with openings for doors are braced at the bottom by SILL IRONS (Illus. 32, page 28). As you cannot fit a sill iron to a carton-board flat, cutting out the openings would weaken the flat without serving any real purpose. Nevertheless, you will need to indicate the exact location of each opening by some method that will be clear even after the flats have been given several coats of paint. The simplest way is to cut rectangles of the grey *chipboard* used for the backs of writing tablets. Make one the size of each opening and glue it over the place where the opening would be if you cut it through the flat. Illus. 49 shows these symbolic openings.

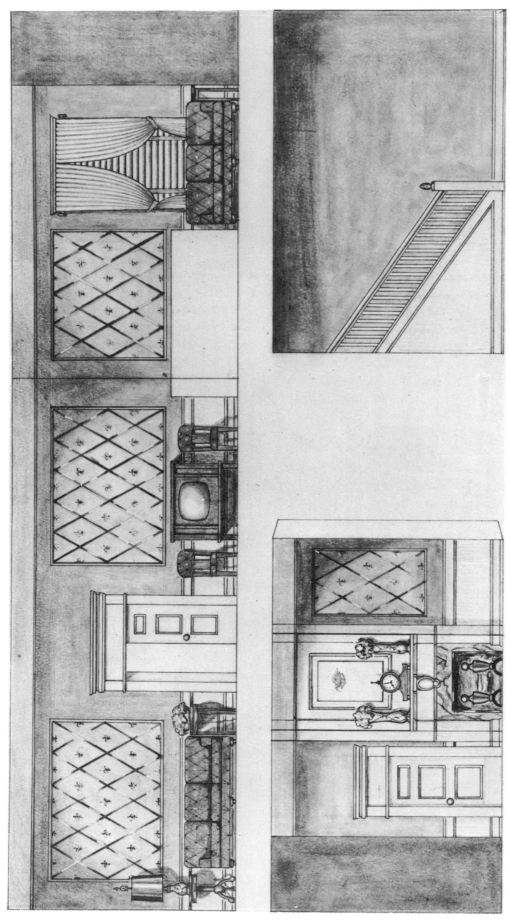

Illus. 46. LAYOUT FOR DISPLAY MODEL. This shows the preliminary drawing for a set made to provide the director, the cast, and the staff with a clear idea of how the set will look. The doors, window, mantelpiece, bookcase, and the furniture along the back wall have all been painted on to save trouble. One door is closed to show that the upstage opening is not merely an archway.

The other door is left open to reveal the stairs, which are painted on the backing. I have made the main set in two parts to fit on this page. However, construction is simpler when all the main walls are painted on one strip. Note that the side backings are not needed in this type of model.

Illus. 47. FINISHED DISPLAY MODEL. This is a more elaborate version made to advertise the play. Both doors and the window have thickness pieces. The stairs in the hall and all the pieces of furniture have been constructed in three dimensions.

In Illus. 50, the "opening" for the fireplace has been painted black. However, the model doors and windows require a more elaborate treatment because their frames are larger than the openings. For example, the opening in the back wall measures 7' high and 4' 4" wide, but the doorframe is 7' 2" high and 5' wide. The solution is to paint doors and windows on chipboard and stick these to the "openings" with double-faced cellophane tape. Illus. 50 shows the finished set.

Hinging. When you are experimenting with arrangements of flats, you will often want to make TEMPORARY BOOKS. This is easily done by running short strips of $\frac{1}{2}$" cellophane tape across the cracks between the flats to act as model hinges (Illus. 51).

When you are ready to paint your flats, you will need to substitute the more permanent arrangement shown in Illus. 52. This shows a strip of 1" *gummed cloth-* or *paper-tape* run vertically along the crack. This serves both as a set of hinges and as a stripper.

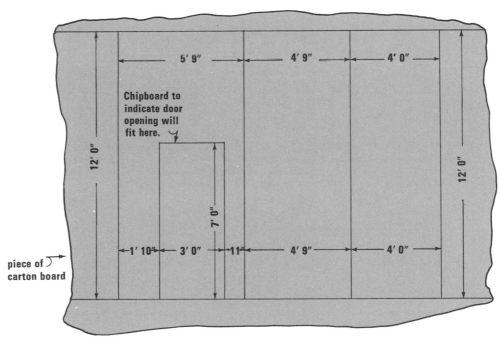

Illus. 48. LAYING OUT FLATS FOR A WORKING MODEL. Carton board is composed of three layers. The inner layer is corrugated. This makes it look like a row of small tubes. The board is much stiffer along the "tubes" than it is across them. As you want your flats to be stiffer the long way, and as all flats are higher than they are wide, cut so the "tubes" will run up and down. Get a piece of carton board wide enough to let you make "tubes" at least 12" long. Rule two parallel lines 12' apart. Use a straightedge, such as a yardstick for this. Draw a line near one edge of the board at right angles to the parallels. Measure the widths of the flats along both the top- and bottom-lines, and mark points. Connect the points for each flat. The result should look like the drawing except that the widths of your flats will probably be different.

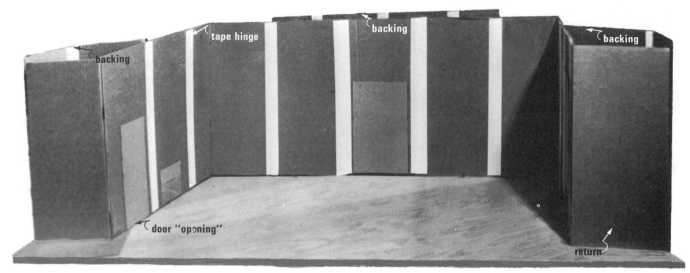

Illus. 49. WORKING MODEL BEFORE PAINTING. This is crude compared to the set in Illus. 47, but it has two important virtues. It can be made quickly and easily, and it lets you experiment as much as you like merely by shifting the flats around and making a few new ones if necessary. Do not cut openings in the flats, but indicate their positions by pasting on rectangles of chipboard. This version does not show the doors and windows that will be added later. Backings are an important part of a working model. Make all of them, including one for the fireplace, and place them in position even though they cannot be seen from the front of the model.

Illus. 50. WORKING MODEL AFTER PAINTING. This shows the model after the doors, the window, and furniture have been added. This is still another version of the set in Illus. 30. Note how much the effect is altered by changing the decoration. The walls in this model were covered with contact paper to save time. A real set would use a slightly simpler design applied with a stencil. That is not as big a job as you may think.

If you use cloth tape, choose the type that must be wet to make it stick. Self-sticking tapes are too stiff, too thick, and too expensive. When gummed tape is not available, you can cut 1″ strips of thin cloth and glue or paste them over the cracks between your flats.

Jiggers. For model jiggers you cannot use carton board. On a 1″ scale, a 3″ jigger is only $\frac{1}{4}$″ wide, and such a narrow strip of carton board would be unmanageable. Jiggers should be $\frac{1}{4}$″ × $\frac{1}{4}$″ strips of white pine or hardboard. Although neither material comes in this size, the strips can easily be cut on a power saw. If you do not have access to such a saw, make your jiggers by cutting out five or six $\frac{1}{4}$″

strips of chipboard. Glue these together with rubber cement and dry them under a weight. The result will be less satisfactory than a wooden jigger, but it will serve (Illus. 53).

Joining Books. Although books of real flats are joined by lashing or nailing, neither can be done with carton board. Substitute procedures are shown in Illus. 54 and Illus. 55. As jiggers always come in the middle of a book, they are never lashed or nailed.

Stiffening. When flats are hinged and lashed, they will normally stand upright but the walls tend to bow. With a real set, lowering the ceiling on to the wall flats helps stiffen the walls, but even more stiffening may be needed. Working models rarely have ceilings, and even if you add one, it will be too light to do any good. Hence, every wall containing more than one flat must be stiffened in some way.

Strips of white pine that measure about $\frac{3}{16}'' \times \frac{3}{4}''$ make ideal STIFFENING BATTENS (Illus. 56). Woodworking shops call these "rippings" and throw them away. If you cannot get rippings, cut two strips of chipboard $\frac{3}{4}''$ wide and glue them together with rubber cement. You will need two battens for each wall. They should be slightly shorter than the width of the wall.

Stiffening battens can be attached temporarily by placing them on the back of the flats and sticking push pins into them from the front. This is similar

to the technique used for lashing or nailing shown in Illus. 54.

For more permanent stiffening, get $\frac{3}{4}''$ double-faced cellophane tape. Stick one side of the tape to the batten. Then press the tape side of the strip against the back of the wall (Illus. 56).

Bracing. Real sets must be braced to keep them from shaking whenever an actor opens or closes a door. Model walls rarely need bracing. However, if necessary, place a block of white pine behind the weak spot and attach the wall to it with a push pin. Or use double-faced cellophane tape between the wall and the block. Either method can also be employed for ground rows or set pieces. One such brace is shown in Illus. 56.

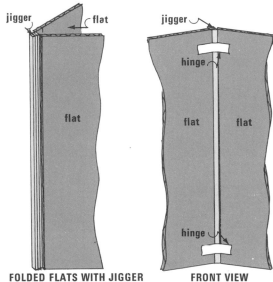

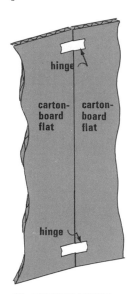

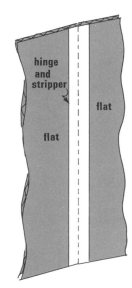

Illus. 51. TEMPORARY HINGES. Two strips of cellophane tape will be sufficient for this purpose.

Illus. 52. PERMANENT HINGE. Make these of gummed cloth- or paper-tape. They also serve as strippers.

Illus. 53. HINGING A JIGGER. The back view shows a jigger made from strips of chipboard. The front view shows temporary hinges in place.

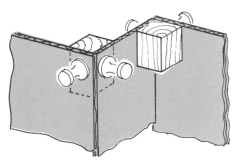

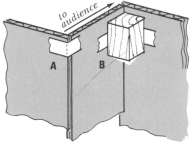

Illus. 54. TEMPORARY CORNER JOINTS. As you will spend a good deal of time experimenting with various arrangements of your model flats, you will need a quick and easy way of joining books at corners. Push pins and small blocks of white pine do very well.

Illus. 55. BOOKS JOINED AFTER PAINTING. When we assemble our books after painting them, any devices used to make joints must be kept on the back. An ordinary corner can be joined with two strips of $\frac{1}{2}''$ cellophane tape (A). This will do whether the real flats are to be lashed, hinged, or nailed. A reverse corner needs two $\frac{3}{4}''$ white-pine blocks like the one at B. Tack a strip of cellophane tape, face out, to the block. Turn the block around and press the tape against the corner made by the flats. When the flats do not meet at a right angle, the blocks must be beveled.

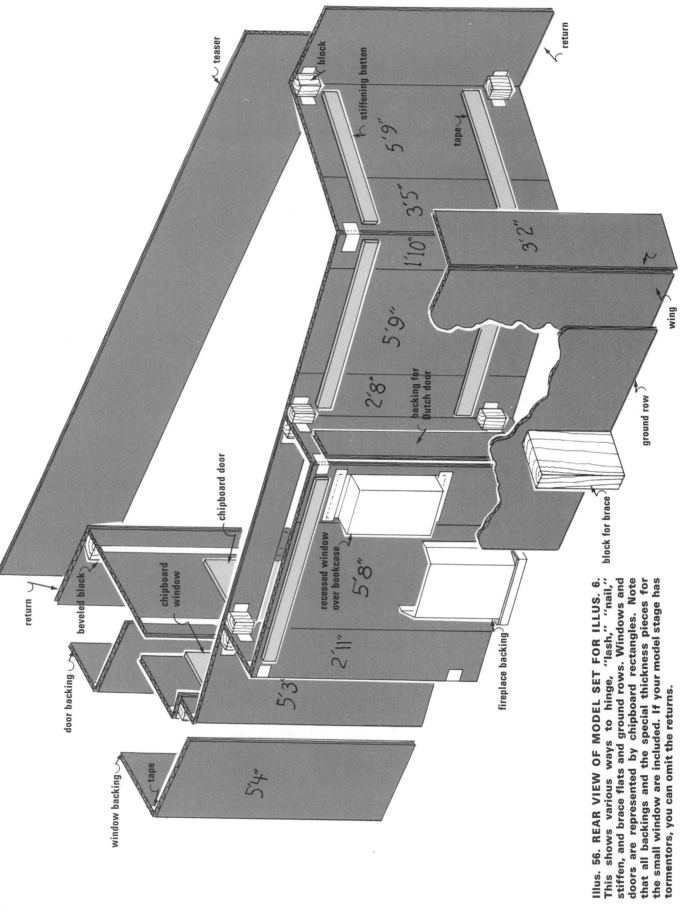

Illus. 56. REAR VIEW OF MODEL SET FOR ILLUS. 6.
This shows various ways to hinge, "lash," "nail,"
stiffen, and brace flats and ground rows. Windows and
doors are represented by chipboard rectangles. Note
that all backings and the special thickness pieces for
the small window are included. If your model stage has
tormentors, you can omit the returns.

Other Units

The suggestions that follow cover virtually every type of unit that you will ever need to build for your working models.

Model Cycloramas. For a drapery cyclorama, use very inexpensive, thin cotton material. Wash it well to remove any trace of stiffness, and iron it to eliminate wrinkles. You will be able to judge the colors of your scenery better if you dye the cyclorama material to match the one on the actual stage you will be using. Cut pieces to scale with *pinking shears* or a *pinking wheel*. Either method makes a zigzag edge that will not ravel, and a hem is unnecessary. Each piece should be a scale version of the real cyclorama. Remember to allow for fullness.

Tack the cloth in folds on strips of wood. Support these on the top of your model stage in the same manner as the strips used to hang the teaser in Illus. 11 (page 15). All hung scenery should be supported in this way.

To make a sky cyclorama, use a large sheet of thin cardboard, or glue two regular-sized sheets together along their short ends. Light blue cardboard is best. However, if you can only get white, paint it a pale, greyish blue. Bend the whole piece in a half circle and place it behind the proscenium of the model stage. The side walls of the stage might hold it in place, but if not, place a vertical strip of white pine on each side of the proscenium. Attach these two strips with push pins pressed through the wall from the front. Spring the cardboard between the blocks. You may need to trim the cardboard or move the blocks to make things fit, but neither adjustment should cause any difficulty.

Drops and Borders. These can be cut from carton board and hung from strips of wood like the teaser in Illus. 11 (page 15). If you make them extra high, you can merely tack them to the strips, rather than hanging them from strings.

However, if the real drop will be only 12′ high, do not paint the model drop higher than 12″. The borders must mask everything above this. If you paint the model drop too high, you may forget that the space above the real drop must be hidden by a border. The same thing applies to model borders. If the real one will be only 6′ high, do not paint the model higher than 6″.

Cutouts. Wings, ground rows, and set pieces can be cut from either carton board or chipboard. Keep them erect by attaching them to blocks of white pine with push pins or double-faced cellophane tape (Illus. 56).

The model wing shown in Illus. 56 is typical. Real wings rarely need bracing, as the flipper keeps the main flat erect. However, if a model wing has a tendency to topple over, add a brace like the one shown with the ground row.

Steps and Platforms. Experimenting with these in working models is much easier when they can be adjusted. There is no way to vary the horizontal dimensions, but you can vary the heights with ease (Illus. 57).

The height of a step is called the RISER and its depth is the TREAD. Virtually all the steps I ever built had 7″ risers and 10″ treads. You need not follow these dimensions, but I can testify that they will be satisfactory in at least nineteen sets out of twenty.

The height of a platform is measured by the number of steps that lead up to it. This means that

Illus. 57. MODEL STEPS AND PLATFORMS. You should be able to adjust the heights of these. Cut blocks of ½″ plywood the size of your platforms. Get heavy chipboard of the kind used to back writing tablets. Cut this to fit your blocks and glue one to each block. Pile up blocks to make a platform as many steps high as you like. This provides an easy way to work out complex arrangements of steps and platforms like the ones shown in Illus. 19, 20, and Illus. 25.

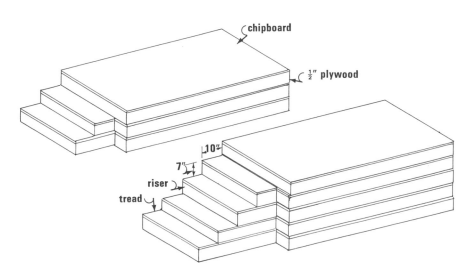

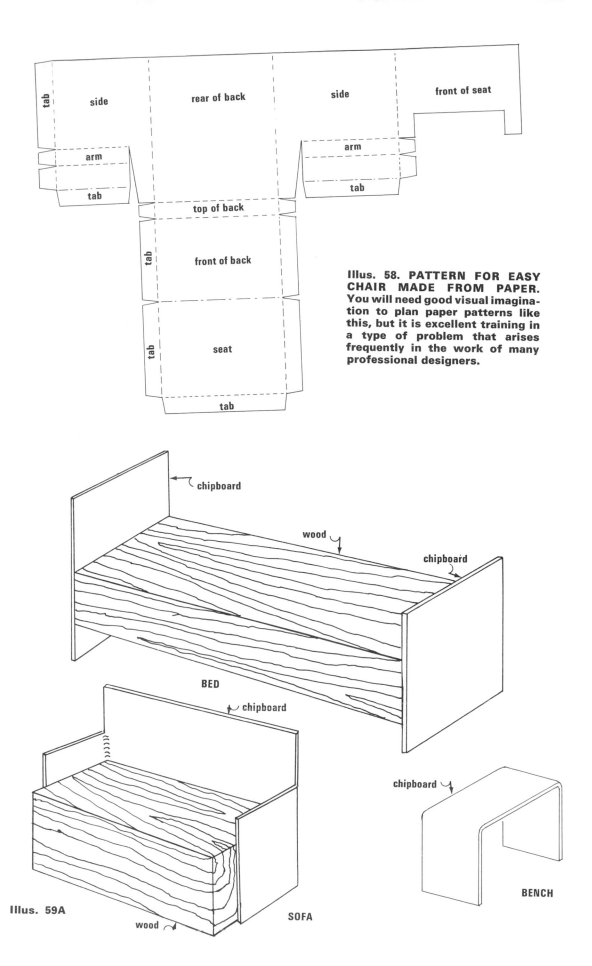

tab

side

rear of back

side

front of seat

arm

arm

tab

tab

top of back

tab

front of back

Illus. 58. PATTERN FOR EASY CHAIR MADE FROM PAPER. You will need good visual imagination to plan paper patterns like this, but it is excellent training in a type of problem that arises frequently in the work of many professional designers.

tab

seat

tab

chipboard

wood

chipboard

BED

chipboard

chipboard

Illus. 59A

wood

SOFA

BENCH

the height of a normal platform is 7″ (one step), 1′ 2″ (two steps), 1′ 9″ (three steps), and so on. As the platform itself makes the top step, stairs leading to a platform contain one step less than the height of the platform. Thus, a platform 2′ 11″ high measures five steps, and the corresponding stairs contain only four steps.

Tree Trunks. You could carve tree trunks from wood or Styrofoam or model them in papier mâché, or modelling clay. However, for working models, three-dimensional tree trunks are not worth even the small amount of trouble that these methods require—a trunk cut out of chipboard and held

erect with a block of wood like the ground row in Illus. 56 will meet every need.

Model Properties

Furniture and other properties for display models can be made by cutting and folding stiff paper (Illus. 58). Properties for working models are another matter entirely. They are tools to help you plan your set. For this purpose, anything roughly the right size and shape will do. The examples in Illus. 59 and Illus. 60 are crude, but they are also ideal. If your working models are fancier than

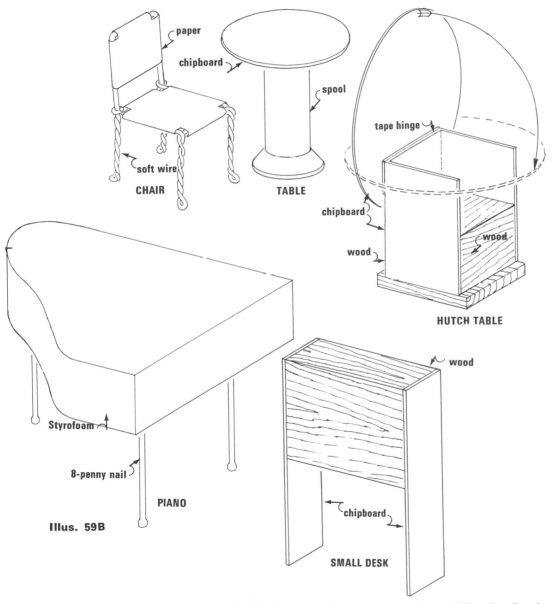

Illus. 59A and 59B FURNITURE FOR WORKING MODELS. The designer of a set like the Greek tent in Illus. 16 (page 18) or the Spanish mission in Illus. 18 (page 20) would design the furniture and have it made by the prop crew. However, such cases are rare. For ordinary sets, you will borrow or rent the furniture. As you cannot decide in advance exactly how it will look, crude models are as useful as fancy ones. Spend your time designing, not in adding unnecessary details to your models.

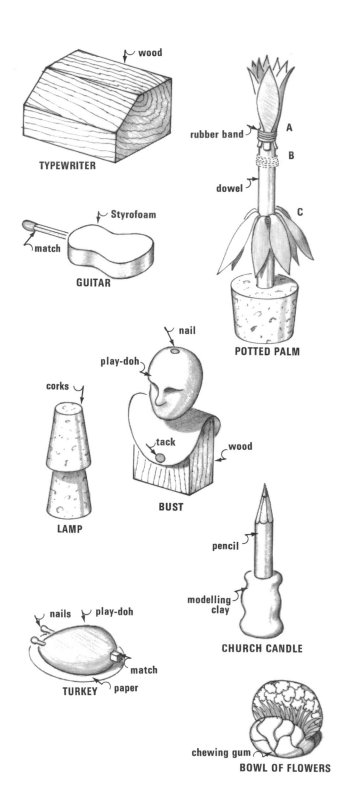

TYPEWRITER

wood

GUITAR

Styrofoam

match

POTTED PALM

rubber band

dowel

A

B

C

LAMP

corks

BUST

nail

play-doh

tack

wood

TURKEY

nails

play-doh

match

paper

CHURCH CANDLE

pencil

modelling clay

BOWL OF FLOWERS

chewing gum

Illus. 60. SMALL PROPS FOR WORKING MODELS. The materials and methods shown here will enable you to make almost any kind of prop that you require for a working model. Do not be finicky. If it takes over ten minutes to make a model prop, you are wasting time. These examples illustrate the wide variety of materials that can be used to construct working props. The only one that needs an explanation is the palm tree. A rubber band is wrapped around the dowel and moved down to Position B. Paper leaves are then arranged around the dowel with their stems downward. The band is pushed over them to Position A. Lastly, the leaves are bent down like those shown at C.

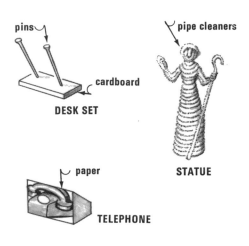

pins

cardboard

DESK SET

pipe cleaners

STATUE

paper

TELEPHONE

on a small prop to add a touch of color, the dab of color should be the right size and the right tone. For example, a single red rose in a vase must be indicated by a tiny spot of red for the rose and spots of green for the leaves.

Enlarging and Reducing

When you do research for scenes like those in Illus. 16 through Illus. 18, you will often find a design which is just what you want except that it is the wrong size and must be enlarged or reduced before you can use it. The usual procedure is to trace the original on tracing paper and divide it into squares. You then draw a similar pattern of larger or smaller squares.

The diagonal method shown in Illus. 61 is much more satisfactory, as the slanting lines help to fix lines when redrawing. Also, there are many other ways to use diagonals for changing proportions. For example, they allow you to make a design wider or narrower without altering its height. If you familiarize yourself with diagonals now, they will be old friends whenever you find a new application for them.

these, you are wasting time on model-making that you should spend on designing.

However, every prop, no matter how small, is an important part of the set and should be represented in some way. You can paint pictures and draperies on the walls, but every free-standing prop should be made. Furthermore, if you are counting

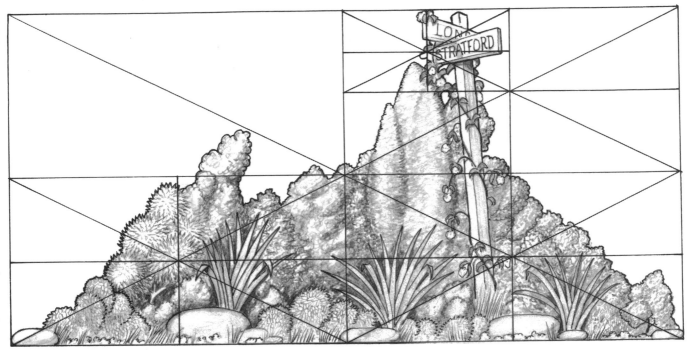

Illus. 61. ENLARGING AND REDUCING. The procedure shown here works for either enlarging or reducing. It is much more satisfactory than the conventional method of ruling squares over the original and then making a similar grid of larger or smaller squares over which the enlarged or reduced version is drawn. With the method shown, the diagonals help to fix lines. Also, you can add extra subdivisions in areas where there are many details.

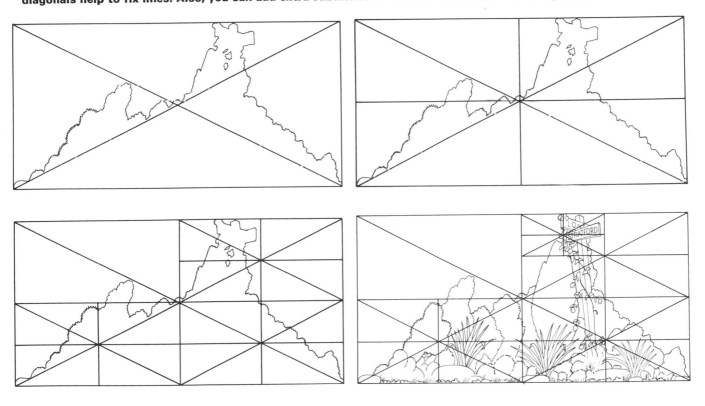

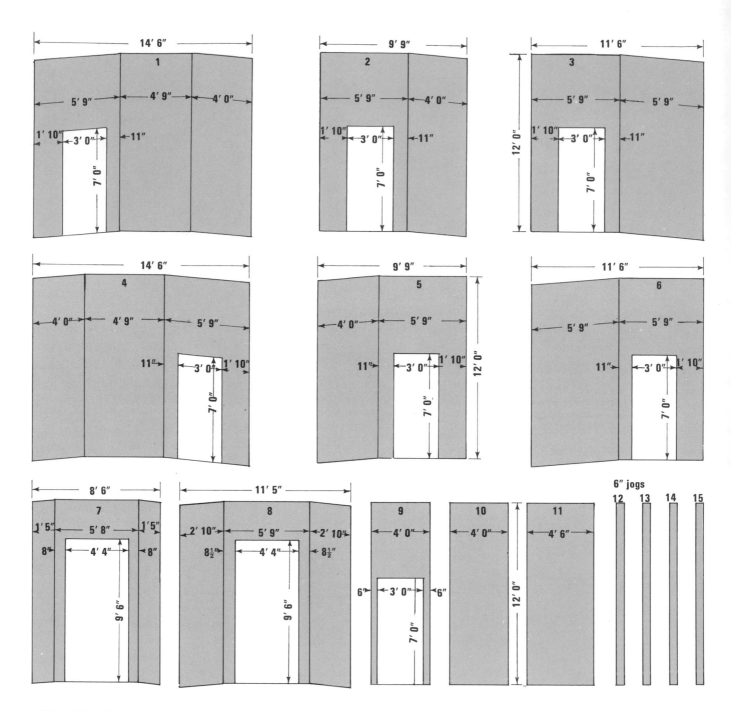

Illus. 62. WALL UNITS FOR A CONVERTIBLE SET. These are front views of the units required for the walls and backings of either a real convertible set or a convertible model. You will also need various accessories, such as doors, windows, steps, platforms, and so on. The numbers on the books identify them in Illus. 63 and help you keep track when you design your own sets.

5. DESIGNING

WITH A MODEL

At first, it may seem that the more freedom a designer has, the easier his work becomes. Actually, too much freedom is a handicap. When I wanted to qualify for Donald Oenslager's class in scene design, he told me to sketch any kind of set. I spent ten times as long deciding what set to choose as I did in designing and drawing the sketch.

Every beginner goes through this. You cannot really start to design a set in your head until you gain some experience. And yet, you need some sort of model that you can see and handle—which means you must make a model before you design it! This may seem contradictory, but it really is not.

I once designed a set in which the flats were permanently hinged and painted. The sizes of the flats and the locations of the openings were planned so that the books could be arranged to suit almost any interior scene as well as many exteriors. However, it was made to fit a 26′ stage. As most school stages are wider, I have worked out the version shown in Illus. 62. This is suitable for a stage where the opening between the tormentors usually measures about 30′.

A full-scale set of this type eliminates many problems that trouble school drama groups. Once the set is built and painted, most plays can be staged without further expense or effort—the set or sets for a play would be available at rehearsal. If the set can be stored on the stage, it can even be used for exercises during courses in Play Production and Acting.

You can build a model of the convertible set in Illus. 62 without designing anything yourself. You can then arrange the parts in various ways until it suits the scene for which you need a model.

When a school owns a convertible set, the design class can work with models of the real one. Full-scale sets can then be arranged to let students see how their designs will look on an actual stage. Needless to say, this provides a strong incentive for students to turn out good work.

Even if your school lacks a convertible set, the advantages of a convertible model make it an almost indispensable tool for beginning designers.

As you must understand the construction and use of the real set before you can understand the model, we shall discuss the real one first.

A Full-Scale Convertible Set

Our problem is to make a set that can be changed merely by rearranging the parts and without re-painting the walls. All the wall units must be built and painted at the same time. If we add a new unit or unhinge an old one, we must repaint the whole set because it is almost impossible to match an old paint job. This all-at-once rule applies only to walls. Doors, steps, and railings are so easy to paint that you can easily redo your whole collection in a couple of hours.

Devices. Convertible sets require certain devices that would not be needed if we built a set for only one show or even if we worked with a set of stock flats that are rehinged and repainted for each production. Illus. 63 shows typical examples.

Plugs. Every book in Illus. 62 includes one flat with an opening. However, many of these must serve as plain walls. Therefore you will need PLUGS like those shown in Illus. 64, 65 and 66. The double-door in Illus. 65 and the window in Illus. 66 have built-in plugs, which is a great convenience. The only drawback here is that if you ever want to add another door or window, you will need to repaint the whole set in order to make the new plug match. You can also make three or four plugs like that in Illus. 64, but 4′ 4″ wide and 2′ 6″ high. These can be used either above doors or below windows. They save repainting flats if you want to add an extra unit, but they make scene shifting more troublesome.

In any case, paint the plugs when you paint the flats, but do not paint them while they are in the flats. If you do, the lips will act like stencils and leave a strip of unpainted canvas around each opening.

Jogs. As our largest books measure only 14' 6", we cannot make a straight wall wider than that without leaving unsightly cracks. The solution is to insert one or more 6" jogs. Such jogs rarely hurt the

looks of the set. In fact, those in the back wall of Illus. 63 might be introduced as a decorative feature to enhance the importance of the middle door.

A jog can also be used to shorten a wall. Thus, the stage-left wall in Illus. 63 measures 14' 6" after combining a jog with an 11' 5" book and a 4' flat.

Overlaps. Flats in ordinary scenery overlap ¾" at the corners so that they can be lashed. In most cases, we can do this with a convertible set as well. However, there are times when the only unit available is too long. If this is part of the back wall,

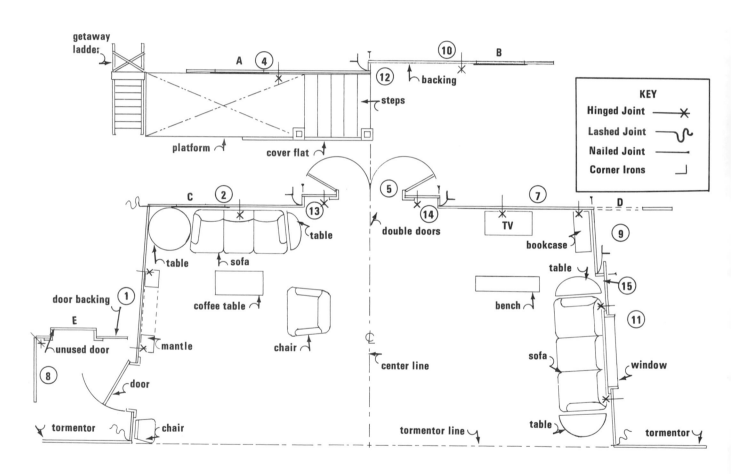

Illus. 63. ARRANGING A CONVERTIBLE SET. This shows most of the devices that you need to make a convertible set fit a variety of floor plans. The set is a 30' version of the one in Illus. 7 and Illus. 30. The numbers in circles refer to Illus. 62. Points A, B, and C indicate plugs used to turn books with openings into solid walls. If you run out of plugs, an opening in a backing can be filled by a door (Point E). This door plays no part in the action. However, the fact that it is masked by the door in Book 1 may keep spectators from noticing it. Book 7 overlaps Flat 9 at Point D, which happens to be on the edge of an opening. Thus, although Book 7 is 14' 6" wide, only 9' 7" of it is visible. Jogs 12, 13, 14 and 15 are

used to make long walls out of two or three books without leaving unsightly cracks in the middle of the wall. The only unit available to take the window on stage left is Book 11. This measures 11' 5", which lacks 3' 1" of completing the 14' 6" wall. Even if the set included a 3' 1" flat, it could not be used without leaving an ugly crack. The solution shown uses Flat 9, which measures 4', and Jog 15. This makes the walls 11¾" too long. To correct this, Book 11 must overlap the jog. That makes a bad joint, but one which is far better than a crack in the middle of a wall. Flats that overlap cannot be joined by lashing. They must be nailed.

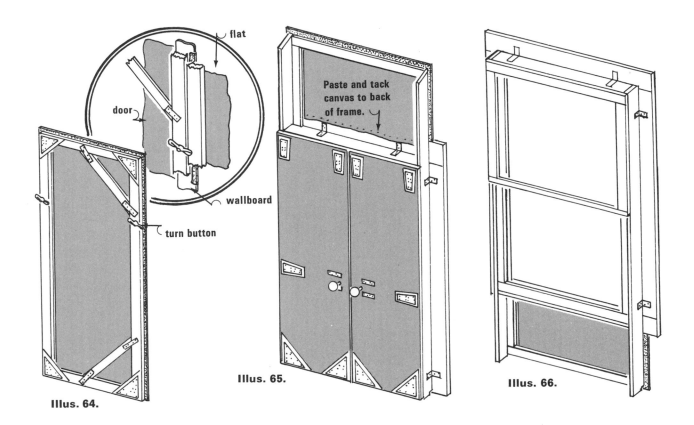

Illus. 64.

Illus. 65.

Illus. 66.

Illus. 64. **PLUG FOR DOOR OPENING.** This shows a plug for a 7′×3′ opening. One for a 9′ 6″×4′ 4″ opening will need a toggle-bar in the center. Lips of wallboard are glued to the sides and top of the frame and extend 1″ past the edges. The canvas is pasted over the lips and wraps around them until it touches the frame. Be sure to paint both the sides and back of the lip. When the plug is in place, it is attached to the flat by two turn buttons. Illus. 65. **PLUG ON DOUBLE DOOR.** As double doors fit 9′ 6″×4′ 4″ openings, they need plugs over them to fill the extra space. These can be built-in like the example, or the plugs can be separate. Illus. 66. **PLUG ON WINDOW.** The gap below a window must be filled by a plug unless it is masked by a sofa or television set. A built-in plug is convenient, but a separate plug can be used.

it can overlap the side wall as much as desired. Book 7 in the up-left corner of Illus. 63 is an example.

Overlapping units cannot be lashed, so they must be nailed. This does not affect a one-set show, but if a scene has to be changed, a stagehand must climb a ladder to pull the top nail. Although this will slow down the scene shift, it does not take long if the action has been properly rehearsed.

When the overlapping unit is part of a side wall, the problem is more serious. The overlap will not mask the crack, and the nails cannot be counted upon to hold the units in close contact. If the crack pulls open and a line of light shows through it, tack a strip of dark canvas to the stile of the cross-stage flat. This will not actually hide the crack if one develops, but it will keep light from shining through (Illus. 67).

Other Units. A real convertible set will need a 32′ × 14′ ceiling, two large (9′ 6″ × 4′ 4″) plugs, at least four small (7′ × 3′) plugs and five or six 6″ jogs. If your stage lacks a plastered backwall that can be painted blue, you will need a blue backdrop as well.

The set should also have three single doors with frames, a double door and frame, a window, and a mantlepiece. Other units, including steps, platforms, and extra doors and windows, can be added as you need them and these can be repainted quickly and easily. (Again, note that adding double doors and windows with built-in plugs means repainting all your flats. See page 47.)

Platforms. As the height of a platform can be adjusted merely by changing the legs (Illus. 33, page 30), you need consider only the dimensions of

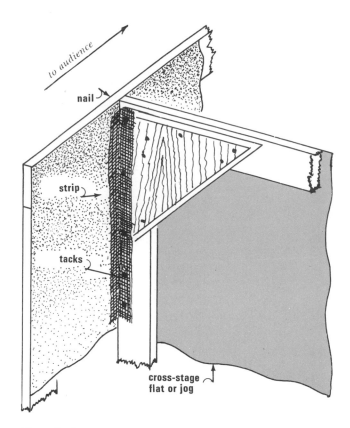

Illus. 67. STRIP TO MASK BAD OVERLAP. When a side wall must overlap a back wall or a jog like No. 15 in Illus. 63, any crack that develops can be seen by the audience. In such cases, tack a flap of dark cloth to the edge of the back wall or the jog. The flap acts as a backing for the crack and helps to keep it from being noticed. Arrange your lights so that they will not shine through the crack. The side wall must be joined to the back wall or jog by nailing (see page 49).

the top. The tops in Illus. 68 were built for one play but could be adapted to almost any scene in which platforms are needed, except those with a special shape.

Steps. Unfortunately, steps cannot be adjusted in any way. In spite of that, ingenuity will often show you how to put old steps to a new use. Suppose you have two sets of stairs, 4' wide. One has five steps and one has three. If you make a 4' × 10' platform six steps high, you can put one set of steps on the platform and create a stairway with nine continuous steps.

Cover Flats. As these are not adjustable, you will need a different one for each platform height and each set of steps. When a cover flat, like that in Illus. 32B (page 28), has a railing, paint the canvas to match the woodwork. This avoids worrying about making it match the wall.

Mantelpiece. The mantel in Illus. 13 (page 17)

is the best type for a convertible set. It can be placed anywhere along a wall and does not need an opening behind it. An almost flat mantel (Illus. 32B, page 28) must come in front of an opening. When the mantel is only a shelf (Illus. 6, page 10) or very shallow (Illus. 32B), it presents a problem.

The lowest opening in our convertible set is 7' high, whereas mantels are rarely over 5'. In such cases, the best solution is to build a shallow chimney breast high enough to mask the opening. Illus. 46 and 47 (pages 36, 37) show such a chimney breast although that set is not convertible. Another plan is to hang a large picture so that it covers all but 6" or 8" of the gap above the mantel. This can be filled with a carton-board plug painted to match the wall as closely as possible. The plug could then be masked with a long, low vase filled with ivy.

If you expect to use many shallow mantels, you can build two of the plugs shown in Illus. 64. Make one 3' 3" × 3' to fit the top of a small opening, and the other 5' 9" × 4' 4" to fit the top of a large opening. Paint them when you paint your set to get a perfect match. When you use one of these, a shallow mantel will give no trouble, but you will still need a chimney breast when the mantel is a mere shelf (Illus. 6, page 10).

Window Backings. As the view through a window never matches the walls of a room, you cannot use your stock flats as window backings. One solution is to omit windows entirely, and this is reasonable—the audience will assume that the missing wall of the set contains windows. Another

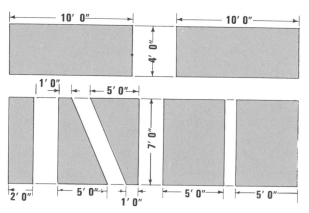

Illus. 68. DIMENSIONS OF PLATFORM TOPS. As you can vary the height of a platform like the one in Illus. 33 merely by changing the height of the legs, the only thing that matters is the size and shape of the top. The platforms shown here will be enough for every set in this book except the one in Illus. 81, and you can use some of them even for that.

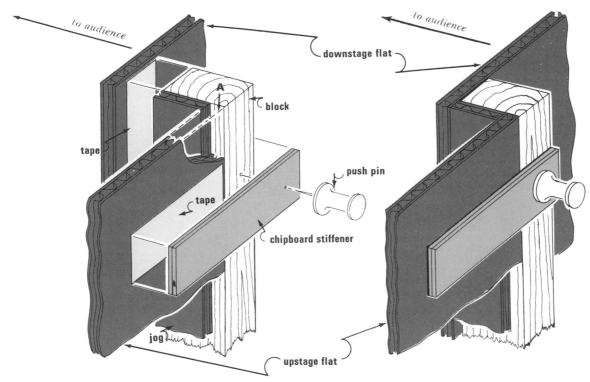

Illus. 69. MODEL JOGS FOR BACK WALLS. When a jog is used in a back wall, both flats must overlap the jog. The left-hand drawing is an exploded view showing the parts before they are put together. The upstage flat has been cut away to show the niche marked A which is the key to the assembly. Provide for this by making the block as wide as the jog (½″) plus the thickness of your carton board. Glue the block to the jog. The drawing on the right shows the parts after they have been joined with two strips of double-faced cellophane tape, a chipboard stiffener, and a push pin.

solution is to treat a window like those used in drapery sets and cover them with black or translucent cloth (Illus. 14 and Illus. 15, page 18). However, the best procedure is to make a special window backing by hinging two 5′ 9″ flats together. If they are painted a pale grey-blue, they will serve for most backings. When you want the backing to represent something special—such as a brick wall outside a window—repainting two flats is a comparatively small job.

A Convertible Model

The methods given in Chapter 4 for constructing and assembling working models apply equally well to convertible models. However, two features deserve particular attention.

Jogs. Although ordinary models rarely include 6″ jogs, almost every set made with a convertible model requires at least one, and a set like Illus. 63 needs four.

A model of a 6″ jog is only ½″ wide and difficult to handle. Therefore it must be stiffened with a block that runs the full height of the jog (Illus. 69). This block also provides an easy means of joining the jog to the adjacent flats.

It is important to make the joints in the model overlap like those in the real set. Study Illus. 69 and Illus. 70 carefully. Note that in back-wall jogs, the block is wider than the jog. However, in side-wall jogs, the jog is wider. This means that you will need two model jogs for each one in your real convertible set.

You do not need separate jogs for the right- and left-hand sides. A right-hand jog becomes a left-hand one simply by turning it upside down.

Plugs. As every convertible book has an opening, you will need model plugs as well as model doors and windows.

The number of such plugs in your set is important. If you have only three small plugs and fail to keep track of them, you may design a set that needs four or more.

Illus. 71 shows the plugs, doors (with frames), and

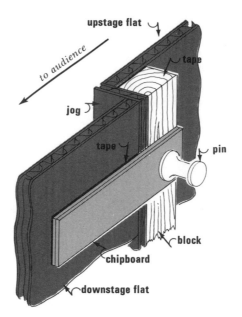
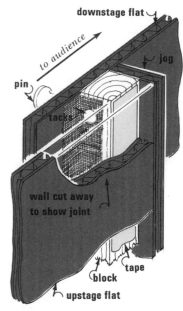

Illus. 70. MODEL JOGS FOR SIDE WALLS. The left-hand drawing shows the normal case where the jog overlaps both flats. The block must then be narrower than the jog by the thickness of the carton board. The right-hand drawing shows a case like the one in Illus. 63 and 67, where we must disguise a bad overlap. Attach the cloth masking strip to the block with tacks.

Offstage View of Model Jog in a Stage-left Wall

Onstage View of Jog in Stage-left Wall with Bad Overlap

windows that you will need for your convertible model. Simply cut these from chipboard, paint them, and attach them to the "openings" in the model books with double-faced cellophane tape. Note that the plugs should exactly fit the openings, but the door frames and window frames overlap at the edges.

A Training Model. If you have a real convertible set available, your model should copy it exactly. However, if you use your model only as a training tool, limit yourself to three 7′ × 3′ plugs, two 9′ 6″ × 4′ 4″ plugs, and four 6″ jogs. The jogs must be duplicates, that is, you will need four back-wall jogs and four side-wall jogs. However, do *not* use more than four jogs in any one set. Also, if you design several scenes for the same show, do not use more than four jogs in all. These limitations make designing more difficult, but they exercise your ingenuity.

Matching Floor Plans

If you start by trying to create an original design, you cannot hope to solve all your problems at once. Fortunately, acting editions of plays usually contain plans of the sets. Most directors want their sets to match the printed versions as closely as possible. If you begin your study of design by trying to make your working model fit printed plans, you will have

a clear idea of what you want to achieve. Furthermore, you will not be faced with problems that cannot be solved without some experience in directing.

A convertible model can be made to match many printed plans almost exactly. In other cases, you must make fairly large changes, and sometimes must design an entirely different set.

Start with plans that you know your model can be made to fit with only minor changes. The sets in Illus. 5 (page 9), 22 (page 22), 73, 74, 78, and 79 meet this requirement. None of them needs more than one large plug, three small ones, and three single doors.

Study Illus. 63 carefully first. This is an almost perfect duplicate of the plan in Illus. 7 (page 12) except that it is 4′ wider. It would be better to avoid the door in the down-right backing and the jog in the stage-left wall, but these are a small price to pay for the convenience and economy of a convertible set.

The set in Illus. 22 (page 22) is a good one to start with as it presents no special problems. Those in Illus. 73, Illus. 74, Illus. 78, and Illus. 79 are also easy. However, in trying to duplicate the last two, you must work from sketches instead of floor plans.

You cannot always match your original this

closely. Illus. 5 provides examples of the features you may need to sacrifice and the additions you must add to make a convertible model fit a plan designed by someone else. There are several possibilities in this case. For example:

Omit both windows. Substitute a bench for the window seat at J.

Omit the beam over the alcove.

Make a special chipboard rectangle to represent the Dutch door and its frame. This is necessary because the convertible set does not include a door of this type. Also, in a real set you would use a stock doorframe. This has an opening only 2′ 8″ wide, and the X-type panels shown in Illus. 6 (page 10) look pinched if the door measures less than 3′. Hence, you must redesign the panels. Furthermore, the door will be moved so far stage right that it cannot be opened without striking the chair at M. Under these circumstances, you may be wise to make the door open off stage.

If you use Book 11 (Illus. 62) for the fireplace wall, the alcove will be 11′ 3½″ wide. As the stock platform is only 10′ long, the extra 1′ 3½″ must be provided by making the settle span the gap. This means that the back "legs" of the settle must be longer than the front ones by the height of the platform.

Book 11 contains a 9′ 6″ × 4′ 4″ opening. Design a shallow mantel and chimney breast to mask this.

Although a bookcase can be faked without an opening, it will be better to omit the one in the original design unless the action of the play demands it.

When other sets in this book can be approximately duplicated with a convertible model, the necessary adjustments are indicated in the captions.

After you have acquired some skill, try fitting your convertible model to the plans in printed plays. You will not always be able to come close to the original, but do not give up until you have made an honest effort. This sort of planning provides invaluable experience.

Originating Designs

When you have mastered a convertible model well enough to match other designers' plans fairly well, you will be ready to attempt a design of your own. Always make your designs suit particular scenes in specific plays. This is actually easier than designing imaginary sets. Also, it trains you to make your designs fit specifications. If you design an imaginary set, you could solve a problem simply by omitting the feature that creates the problem, and this teaches you to be a bad designer, not a good one.

A one-act play is your best choice unless you are already familiar with a longer play. Long plays, even those that require only one set, take a good deal of study; if you design your set to suit the action in the first act, it may not fit situations in the seond or third acts. You will not become expert until you can handle long plays. In the beginning, however, you should spend most of your time designing and devote only the necessary attention to studying the play.

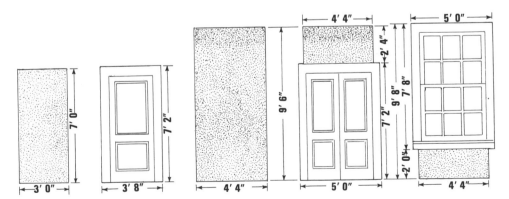

Illus. 71. MODEL PLUGS, DOORS, AND WINDOWS. Cut these from chipboard. Paint them, and fasten them over the chipboard rectangles that represent openings in your model flats. This can easily be done with strips of double-faced cellophane tape.

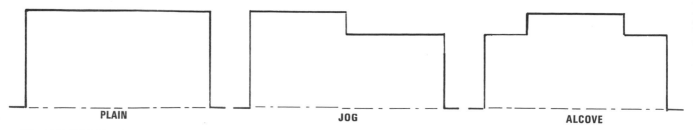

PLAIN   JOG   ALCOVE

Illus. 72. BASIC SHAPES FOR SETS. Almost every interior you ever design will fit one or another of these fundamental floor plans. Any design that fails to fit is apt to degenerate into a formless set like the one in Illus. 10 (page 15).

Basic Shapes. Irregular sets like that in Illus. 10 (page 15) form a crude semicircle. All well-designed sets take one of three basic shapes: PLAIN, JOG, and ALCOVE (Illus. 72).

Variations. Many variations of these basic patterns are possible—a set can be parallel or raked. When it rakes, it can slant either right or left. Rakes of less than 10 degrees or more than 25 degrees rarely look well, but any angle between these limits can be used.

Combinations. An alcove can be added to what is essentially a jogged set (Illus. 73) or a second alcove to a set that already has one (Illus. 5, page 9). This makes the plan more complex and provides more room in a set that would otherwise be overcrowded. Thus, the alcove in Illus. 73 helps to suggest that the set represents a huge room which extends off stage on both sides.

Corners. If the stage is shallow, lopping off one corner of the set may help (Illus. 74). This can also be done when you have nothing to put in the corner and want to avoid empty space.

When you are not confined to stock flats, you may occasionally want to round off one or more corners (Illus. 75). However, curved corners are not recommended unless your building carpenters are experienced.

The Short Wall. Every raked set has one short wall. Normally, it should be placed on the direct axis as it is in Illus. 5 (page 9). This arrangement is unrealistic, but it is certainly the most practical way to keep most of the set on axis and still avoid bad sightlines on the short side.

However, there are two reasons why you may decide to place the short wall on the set axis (Illus. 76). Having all the walls at right angles emphasizes

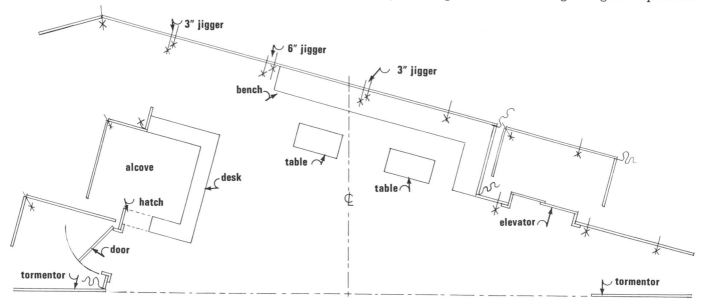

Illus. 73. SET TO SHOW A ROOM THAT IS LARGER THAN THE STAGE. This is made to look like a huge room by extending it off stage in the up-right and down-left corners. Adding an alcove to what is basically a jogged set also makes the room seem larger. The reverse jog lets the set run off stage-left without introducing unsolvable sightline problems. When you try to match this with the convertible model, use a plain wall instead of the stage-right alcove and move the clerk's desk further onstage. The elevator will require specially built sliding doors.

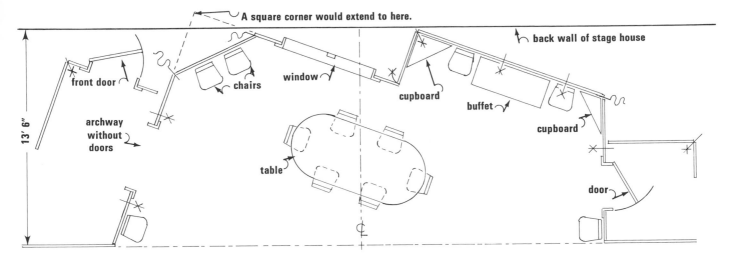

Illus. 74. DINING ROOM SCENE FOR SHALLOW STAGE. By lopping off one corner of this set, I was able to get it on a stage only 13' 6" from the tormentor line to the back wall of the stage house. A square corner would have made this set 1' 4" deeper. I worked for five years on a stage where those extra inches made all the difference between a fine set and an impossible one.

The slanting wall also gave me room to put two chairs where actors can sit without masking each other. Your convertible model can match this neatly if you substitute your single window for the double one. However, the set will be 14' 6" deep, and cutting off the corner will not save any space.

the realism of the scene. It also provides room for some bulky piece of furniture that must be present but which you would like to put where it will not take up valuable playing space. Often, both reasons apply to the same scene. The short wall in Illus. 76 is a good example. Note that although more than half of the secretary's desk will be hidden from some spectators, all of them can see that it is a desk. Furthermore, an actor sitting at the desk, or even sitting on it, will be in plain view of everyone.

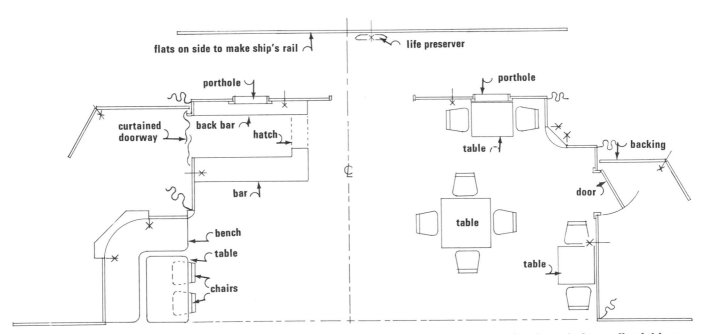

Illus. 75. PLAN FOR A SHIP'S SMOKING ROOM. One or two curved corners, a couple of portholes, a flat laid on its side for a rail, and a life preserver make this obviously a scene on shipboard. If you omit the curved corners, you can duplicate this with your convertible set without repainting any stock units. However, that means building special units for the rail, doorway, and portholes. Do not try it with your model unless you need a shipboard scene for an actual play.

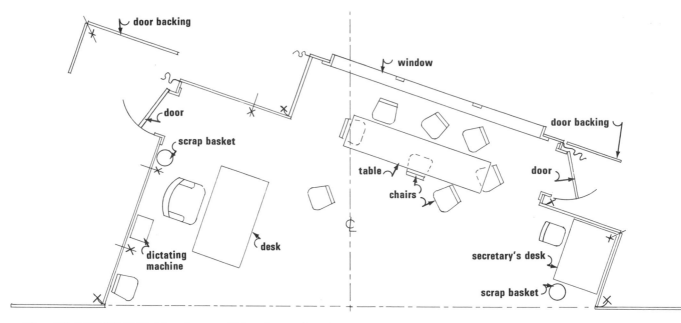

Illus. 76. OFFICE SET. The short wall has been placed on the set axis. This adds realism. It also provides room for the secretary's desk without taking up valuable playing space. A version made with convertible model must be content with a single window. My plan requires no less than five overlaps. Can you find a way to use less?

When your only reason for putting the short wall on the set axis is a need for realism, it is still a good idea to fill the blind corner with some bulky prop such as a cupboard or a filing cabinet. Without this, spectators may wonder subconsciously why this wall is left bare, and why no action takes place in that corner.

Most stage sets are much larger than the rooms they represent. However, you must occasionally show a room which is larger than the stage. This can be done by omitting the short wall and making the set extend into the wings (Illus. 73).

If you do this with a normal alcove set or one where the jog is placed in the usual way, it will be virtually impossible to keep spectators on the far side from seeing into the wings. The solution is to

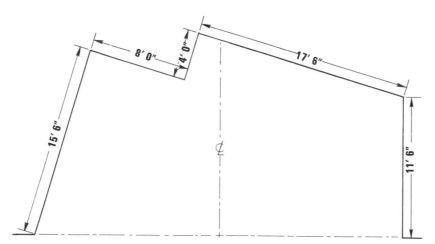

Illus. 77. PLAN TO SHOW OPPORTUNITIES FOR VARIETY. At first sight, the sets in Illus. 78-81 have nothing in common. Nevertheless, they all fit the plan shown here exactly. Although the furniture and decorations have some effect, the real differences are in the sizes, locations, and treatments of the openings. Note how much stairs add to the sets in which they are used. This plan has no special virtues. I give it merely to demonstrate that changes like those in Illus. 78-81 can entirely alter the appearance of a setting even when the basic plan remains the same.

Illus. 78. ROOM IN EXCLUSIVE CLUB. The ponderous mantelpiece, the heavy, leather-covered furniture, and the dark tones of the portraits all work together to tell the audience that members of this club are wealthy, stodgy, and ultraconservative. You will need to substitute a different window and a different mantelpiece when you try to match this with your convertible model. You must also use two 6" jogs and change the proportions of the walls slightly.

Illus. 79. WAYS TO WORK IN MORE OPENINGS. The stairs not only add an interesting level but also let us put an opening behind the love seat. Most sets leave the downstage center area bare. By grouping two doors behind this, we avoid masking either one and still have room at the sides for furniture. Your convertible model will match this almost exactly.

Illus. 80. CASTLE INTERIOR. Although the stonework is the most obvious difference between this and the sets in Illus. 78 and 79, the locations, sizes, and treatments of the openings also play important roles.

Illus. 81. ORIENTAL STREET SCENE. This is another, and entirely different set, that fits the plan in Illus. 77 exactly. The winding stairs create both an impression of height and an air of Oriental mystery. Note that I have managed to get seven openings into this setting. A convertible set would not be much use here. However, a group with a fair-sized stock of separate flats that can be rehinged and repainted for each show could make the walls by adding the two arches. If the platforms in Illus. 68 (page 50) are also available, even the complex stairway would not require building many special units. This set makes a good exercise for the advanced student.

use a reverse jog like the one in Illus. 73. This brings the back wall so close to the tormentor that masking the wings creates no real problem.

Openings. The locations, sizes, and shapes of doors, windows, and fireplaces have a profound effect on the appearance of the scene. Although the four sets on pages 57 and 58 look entirely different, they all fit the basic floor plan in Illus. 77. To a large extent, these differences are due to changes in the openings.

When you work with a convertible model, you can make some alterations by switching doors and windows for plugs. Usually, however, you must rearrange the books. Thus, although Illus. 78 and Illus. 79 both fit the plan in Illus. 77, moving the openings will force you to put every book in a different position.

Steps and Platforms. Even a one-step platform like that in Illus. 5 (page 9) can alter the appearance of a scene. An entire flight of stairs changes the whole effect. However, there are so many other reasons for adding steps and platforms that you will probably never include them merely for the sake of variety.

Ceilings. Sloping ceilings over alcoves completely change the appearance of a set. Ceiling beams are rarely worth the trouble of building them, as few spectators pay much attention to anything above the heads of the actors. Nevertheless, I once helped to construct a set where the ceiling was supported on huge stone arches. The result repaid the effort.

Furniture. The choice and arrangement of furniture makes an enormous difference in the way a set looks. Here again, there are so many other things to consider that a desire for variety is rarely a major factor. The locations of furniture are so closely connected with the locations of openings that you can rarely alter one without altering the other.

Painting. Obviously, the way the walls of a set are painted has a profound effect on its appearance. Few schools will want to repaint a set for every show. Hence, when designing a scene for a school play, you should paint your model to match your school's set. In all other cases, however, you have a free choice of colors and patterns. Take advantage of this by repainting your model each time you design a fresh setting.

Dressing. We DRESS a set when we select draperies, pictures, and the small props such as books, vases, and flowers that go to complete the stage picture. This is so important a job that set dressers for films often receive screen credit.

Most items of set dressing can be painted on the walls of a working model. Props placed on tables or in the middle of the stage are more troublesome, but every one should be included. A single small prop can be as significant as all the rest of the set put together. Suppose, for example, that a scene must represent a shack in which everything, including the furniture, is made of rough, unpainted planks grey with age. One red flower in a tin cup will change the whole stage picture. The flower introduces a touch of color and also tells the audience that at least one character in the play has some feeling for beauty.

Illus. 82. THE SEESAW PRINCIPLE. Imagine the shaded sofa and chair on a seesaw that is pivoted at the center of the stage. Although the sofa is much heavier, the chair counterbalances it because the sofa is on the short arm of the seesaw and the chair is on the long arm. We can rarely balance items by pairs in this way. Instead, we must make everything on one side balance everything on the other. Note also, that what counts is "visual weight," not actual weight.

6. THE PRINCIPLES OF DESIGN

Artists have been creating designs for thousands of years. Experience has taught them that pleasing designs tend to have certain qualities in common, and that designs which lack these qualities are usually unsatisfactory. As a result, there are certain principles to guide the designer. These are not laws—a design is not good because it follows all the principles, nor is one that violates a principle necessarily bad. Nevertheless, there is no doubt whatever that an understanding of the principles will increase your chances of creating successful designs.

If you try to create a design with no guide except your own taste, the results are unlikely to be satisfactory. You must remember you are not making the design to please yourself but to please your audience. Your taste may be better than that of any individual spectator, but unless you satisfy most of them, the design will fail. We all make mistakes. A designer who relies entirely on his own judgment often makes mistakes that he could have avoided. Everyone who works in the theatre must constantly remind himself that the audience is *always* right. A design, like a play, which does not please the audience is a dead loss.

Balance

Many people are irritated by pictures that are not hung straight. The picture itself may be beautiful, but if the frame is crooked, the total effect will be unpleasant. On the other hand, even when the frame is level, you can still be annoyed by a picture that does not BALANCE within the frame. A stage set is always level, but the set may be badly out of balance unless the designer is careful to avoid it.

Everything in a scene appears to have a kind of weight. This weight is more apparent than real. A stage rock may be largely chicken wire and canvas, but it seems heavy to the spectators because they accept it as solid stone.

Furthermore, judgment of weight in a design is

not strictly logical. An object may affect us as being "heavy" even when we know it is light. Thus, anything dark seems heavier than if it were pale or if it were brightly lit. For example, the set in Illus. 30 (page 27) is in balance, but if you put cream-colored slip covers on the furniture stage right and used dark materials for the sofa and draperies stage left, the left side would seem much "heavier."

Interest also increases an object's "weight." A picture weighing only a few ounces can add greatly to the "weight" of a wall. In fact, we can often balance a set by adding a picture on the "light" side. Subtle adjustments can be made by substituting one picture for another. If the new one is slightly larger or darker, it will add a little weight to the side on which it is hung.

Estimating the "weight" of an item is not difficult —anything that seems "heavy" to you will also seem "heavy" to your audience.

The Seesaw. The easiest, and dullest, way to achieve balance is to make a set symmetrical. Then, each side is a mirror image of the opposite side. Although few sets show perfect symmetry, cases like Illus. 23 (page 23) and 30 (page 27) are common. The basic plans are symmetrical, the centers are clearly defined, and the items on one side balance those on the other.

Symmetry is impossible with a raked set. If the set in Illus. 30 were on a slant, it would cease to be symmetrical. It would also cease to balance unless a number of adjustments were made.

Fortunately, symmetry is not needed for balance. What is known as OCCULT, or HIDDEN, BALANCE works like a seesaw. A light object near the side of the set seems to be on the end of the seesaw and will balance a heavy object near the center (Illus. 82).

A set should balance when there are no actors present. As the presence of actors changes the stage picture, problems of balance are introduced, but these concern the director. When a set balances, a competent director can balance the actors. But if the set itself is lopsided, the director will have to fight it all through the scene.

Stability. Sets sometimes present the curious effect of being about to float away. This tends to become stronger when you add actors and may be serious when more than five or six characters are present.

The director must stabilize his stage picture by placing actors in one or both downstage corners. However, he cannot do this without providing reasons for the characters in the play to move to these corners. The designer should furnish such reasons by putting a chair, or a chair and a small desk, in both downstage corners whenever he possibly can. If there is no room for a seat, try to have a door near the corner. A director can usually find some reason for placing a character near the door.

Emphasis and Subordination

In most types of design, we must emphasize one feature, give a little stress to a few others, and deliberately suppress the rest. This can raise major problems. Emphasis is much less important in scene design. Normally, you want to concentrate interest on the actors and keep it off the scenery. *Any set that competes with the actors for attention is bad.*

Occasionally, a set may have some feature of such importance that the designer is tempted to stress it. This is rarely justified. We almost never show an important object throughout a whole scene. Usually, an item is significant only while the actors are speaking of it, looking at it, or touching it. At such times, the actors focus enough attention on the object. If it attracts interest at other times, it does so at the expense of the actors.

For these reasons, avoid strong emphasis on any one point and distribute what emphasis there is over several different items. In Illus. 30 (page 27), for example, the central door and the two groups of furniture are all equally prominent.

On the other hand, it is often necessary to subordinate some item which might otherwise be too conspicuous. Real roses, for example, seem too vivid under stage lights—they distract attention and appear to be artificial. This can be corrected by spattering them lightly with dark paint.

The edges of the platforms in Illus. 25 (page 24) are straight lines, which prevents them from looking like a natural bank of earth. I could not avoid this entirely, but I did hide some of the lines with chicken-wire rocks and camouflaged the rest with paint.

Design Elements

We can think of a set as being made up of walls, doors, furniture, and so on, or as a pattern of abstract design elements.

Lines. The lines in a set may be actual lines painted on the scenery (note the repeated diagonals

Illus. 83. SHAPES. These were traced from my sketch in Illus. 18 (page 20). Although every shape is different, they form two obvious groups. All the shapes in a group harmonize while the groups contrast sharply with each other.

in Illus. 47 on page 37). Usually, however, they are the outlines of objects. The lines you choose make a great deal of difference in the appearance of the stage picture.

Lines can be straight or curved. Straight lines can be horizontal, vertical, or diagonal. Those in Illus. 30 (page 27) are strongly horizontal. Most amateur sets are too low to permit much vertical stress, but Illus. 25 (page 24), 80, and 81 give some

idea of what is possible. Every raked set introduces diagonal lines, as does a stairway. Although every line of the steps in Illus. 80 is actually horizontal or vertical, the long flight itself strikes a diagonal note. This is so strong that it easily balances the great archway in spite of the fact that the stairs are painted to match the walls.

Curved lines permit infinite variations. Compare those in Illus. 2, 18, 23, 25, 78, and 81.

When lines help a design, you should *stress* them by making them *contrast* with their backgrounds, as the curves of the drapery contrast with the sky in Illus. 23 (page 23) and the lines of the trees in Illus. 25 (page 24). On the other hand, when the demands of realism force you to introduce undesirable lines, *subordinate* them by *avoiding* contrasts. The furniture in Illus. 50 (page 38) is as insistently horizontal as that in Illus. 30 (page 27). Nevertheless, the lines are softened to a point where their horizontal effect goes almost unnoticed.

Lines can harmonize and contrast as well as colors. Straight lines harmonize with each other, especially when they are parallel. At the same time, verticals contrast with horizontals, and diagonals contrast with both. Cover the stairway in Illus. 30, and you will see that the design becomes more harmonious. A director could achieve the same effect by having an actor close the doors. Also, compare the set in Illus. 30 with that in Illus. 47 (page 37). Although the two designs are basically alike, the diagonals in the latter give it a very different atmosphere.

Try to make most lines in a set harmonize first and then introduce a few contrasts to avoid monotony. In Illus. 23 the deep curves all resemble each other. This is harmonious, but it would be tiresome if it were not for the hard, straight lines at the top and bottom of the balustrade.

Shapes. If you were to photograph a set and cut out the print along its main outlines, you would have a series of SHAPES. The shapes in Illus. 83 were traced from the adobe chapel in Illus. 18 (page 20). The fact that spectators are rarely aware of shapes makes them an extremely subtle device for harmonizing the parts of a design.

One way to unify a design is to repeat the same shape in different sizes and positions. Thus, in Illus. 23, the draperies, the urns, and the balusters all have approximately the same shape. This is then inverted and used for the trees and the dancer's skirt.

Shapes are not confined to actual objects. They may be the spaces between objects. In Illus. 25 (page 24), for example, the trees suggest Gothic arches because the empty spaces draw the eye more than the trees themselves.

Lines are closely related to shapes, but harmony of line and harmony of shape are not the same thing. In Illus. 84, every possible line has a graceful curve. While these lines harmonize, most of the shapes that they outline do not. Compare this with Illus. 18 (page 20), where both the lines and the shapes are harmonious.

Volume and Mass. If you think of an object as being solid, you become conscious of its VOLUME and MASS. Volume is important in painting and sculpture but plays little part in scene design except in cases where we are able to create a convincing illusion of depth. Illusions of mass are easier to achieve. The two main tree trunks in Illus. 25 look ponderous. Actually, they are light enough to be handled by a girl. From the standpoint of abstract design, mass

Illus. 84. MEANINGLESS CURVES. This type of decoration was popular a hundred years ago. The curves are used merely to be fancy and have no relation to the structure of the doors and furniture. Also, in spite of the fact that the curves harmonize with each other, they do not outline harmonious shapes. Compare the versions in Illus. 30, 47, and 50.

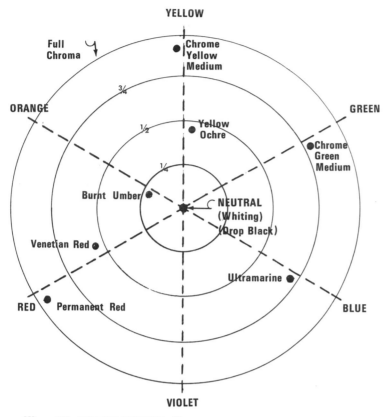

Illus. 85. COLOR WHEEL. Hues are represented as positions around the wheel. Chroma is shown by the distance from the hub. Thus, all shades of grey are in the center while the most vivid colors lie at the extreme rim. The black dots indicate the hues and chromas of the pigments I prefer for scene painting.

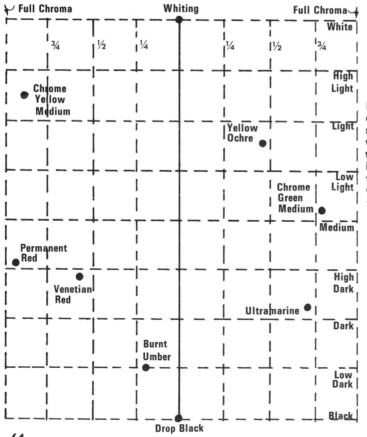

Illus. 86. VALUE AND CHROMA CHART. We cannot conveniently show all three qualities of a tone on the same chart. This one omits hues but locates values vertically and represents chromas by their distance from the neutral (grey) line in the middle. The word "medium" in the names of pigments is used merely to distinguish them from others of similar hues. It has nothing to do with "medium" values. You can forget it except when you order scene paints.

is important because it controls the balance in the stage picture.

Tone. The term TONE covers all colors and also white, black, and the various shades of grey. All tones are related—in fact, all tones can be arranged in a three-dimensional diagram known as the TONE SOLID (Illus. 85 through Illus. 88). This diagram is the key to understanding tones. Your ability to mix paint and to use color schemes will depend largely on how familiar you are with the diagram and your ability to apply it in practice.

Hue. HUE refers to distinctions like those between red, green, and blue (Illus. 85). Although each one blends into those next to it, normally only six hues are considered, including orange, green, and violet. To be more accurate, intermediate hues, such as yellow-green, blue-green, blue-violet, and so on, should be included.

Chroma. We measure the CHROMA, or INTENSITY, of a tone by how far it is from neutral grey. Thus, the outer circle in Illus. 85 represents the various hues at full chroma. Ordinarily, five levels of chroma are enough. For example, we may have grey, red at $\frac{1}{4}$ chroma, red at $\frac{1}{2}$ chroma, red at $\frac{3}{4}$ chroma, and red at full chroma. The brightest ordinary paints and dyes represent full chroma. Day-glow colors would lie outside our circle, but these are rarely used on scenery.

Chroma explains the difference between red and chestnut. When we reduce the chroma of red, we get chestnut. Many people think of brown as a separate hue. Actually, the browns and tans are merely low chromas of hues between red-orange and yellow.

Value. This is the difference between white, grey, and black. VALUES, like hues and chromas, merge into one another. However, it is enough to recognize seven values between white and black (Illus. 86).

Values are not restricted to greys. Every colored tone also has a value. Most bananas, for example, are yellow at $\frac{3}{4}$ chroma and "light" in value.

A hue can reach full chroma only at one particular value. Thus, red is most vivid at "high dark." If we try to make it paler, it turns pink. If we darken red, it becomes maroon. Illus. 87 shows the value at which each hue can reach full chroma. This is worth knowing when you mix paint—if you try to mix a dark vivid orange, you will get brown!

The Tone Solid. Even if you are blessed with a natural eye for color, you will be able to handle it much more easily and successfully if you understand it. When you can visualize the TONE SOLID in Illus. 88 and locate any tone at the correct point in the solid, you will be able to think in terms of tones. Without this, you must handle tones by intuition, which is both less efficient and less effective. Learning to think in terms of the tone solid may take work, but it will be worth every minute you spend on it.

Tone Harmonies and Contrasts. Tones that are close together on either the color wheel or the value chart tend to harmonize. Those far apart contrast with each other. This makes it comparatively easy to provide as much harmony or contrast as you need.

Suppose the walls of your set are blue of "medium" value and $\frac{3}{4}$ chroma. The trim is pale cream (orange at "high light" with only enough chroma to distinguish it from grey). If you feel that the contrast is too great, you could make the blue slightly lighter, greyer, or greener. Or you could make the cream a trifle darker, yellower, or give it a little more chroma. If you prefer greater contrast, you could reverse these procedures.

The whole stage is normally lit in the same tone by colored lights. This mixes with every tone in the scenery, props, and costumes, bringing them nearer together on the color wheel and automatically increasing the over-all harmony. Like magic, sets which look harsh and crude under work lights suddenly become beautiful when the stage lights are turned on. However, you should not count on this, especially if the lighting equipment of your stage is less than ideal.

Learning to Use Tones. Anyone seriously interested in choosing and mixing tones can find many helpful suggestions in books. However, as in most other fields, experience is the best teacher. The late Felix Mahony devised a method of gaining experience with a minimum of trouble. His procedure is explained in Illus. 89. It will not enable you to master tones overnight; you must color dozens, or even hundreds, of designs before you become expert, but the result will be well worth the effort.

Merely coloring simple designs is good practice in handling a brush and learning how paint works on paper. Use this exercise to increase your ability to think in tones, to enlarge your knowledge of color harmonies and contrasts, and to improve your taste. Give serious thought to each example. Do not put one aside until you have done your best to determine which elements are good, which are bad, and how the color scheme could be bettered.

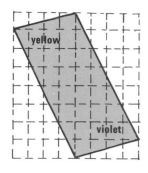

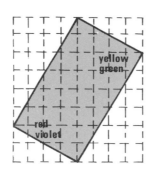

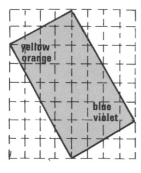

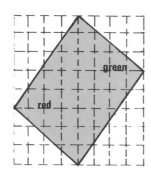

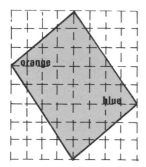

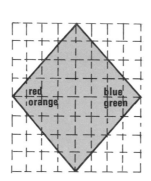

Illus. 87. VALUES AT FULL CHROMA. A tone can reach full chroma at only one value, and no more than two hues reach full chroma at the same value. The shaded area in each of these charts represents the tones that can be obtained with two hues that lie on opposite sides of the color wheel. Such hues are said to be complementary. Mixing a pair of perfectly pure complementary colors would produce neutral grey. Tones outside the shaded areas do not exist. No pigment or mixture of pigments will create a vivid dark yellow or a brilliant pale violet.

Illus. 88. THE TONE SOLID. The charts in Illus. 85 and 87 are actually different views of the same three-dimensional diagram known as the tone solid. This is hard to visualize because its shape is both unfamiliar and unsymmetrical. Illus. 85 is a top view. The charts in Illus. 87 are vertical cross-sections. Try to visualize Illus. 88 as a hollow cylinder with the charts arranged around the white-black axis like the spokes of a wheel. Each chart makes two spokes.

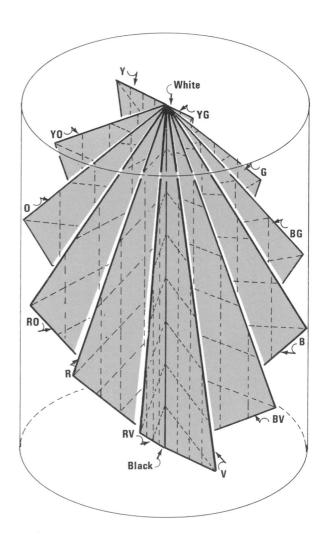

Illus. 89. THE MAHONY SYSTEM FOR STUDYING DESIGN IN TONE. Trace one of these designs on tracing paper. Place artist's carbon paper over cheap water-color paper. Lay your tracing on this and make a copy by re-tracing your design. Prepare many such copies of the same design and paint each one with a different color scheme. Work systematically. Start with only two tones. Choose one as a base and paint the shaded area with this. Paint the unshaded area in one copy yellow, in another yellow-orange, in a third orange, and so on. Then try a series in which your base tone is combined with each of the seven values of one hue. Try another series that contrasts the base tone with the four chromas of another hue when all four have the same value. Examine your results. Decide which ones are good and which are ugly. Do not worry about realism in selecting tones, but consider it in the result. Is a green tree on a blue background more attractive than a dark red tree on a yellow background? Will your answer be the same if the tree is pale pink? Try three tones on the areas outlined by the solid lines. Do vivid tones go best in large areas or in small ones? Is it better to use bright red on the whole lion or restrict it to his claws and his tongue? Will your opinion be the same if the tone is bright blue? Add a fourth tone on the areas separated by the dotted lines. What effects does this have? Merely coloring designs will not teach you much. You must train yourself to think in terms of tone combinations. Learn the effect of each one and what changes would make it more harmonious or more striking.

Studying color by the Mahony System may seem like a slow process, but it is much quicker than trying to master tone design by painting models or sketches. You will learn as much from each exercise as you would from one model, and you can color 20 or 30 designs in less time than it would take you to paint a model.

By working with the Mahony System, you can find out whether or not you have enough serious interest in color to achieve real success. If you discover that the exercises become more and more fascinating as you proceed, you have an excellent chance of attaining sufficient skill to put you at the professional level. On the other hand, if the work bores you, it will probably be wiser to consider some field of design where color is not a major factor.

Unity and Variety

Books on art theory usually mention UNITY and VARIETY as basic principles. They are important, and you need practical examples of how to combine unity and variety in the same design.

Too little variety makes a design dull, whereas too little unity makes one BUSY or meaningless. The solution does not consist in finding some middle ground where unity and variety balance but in adding as much of both qualities as you can. Although they sometimes conflict, many cases occur where you can increase one without decreasing the other.

In Illus. 23 (page 23), for example, the drapes are dark red, the yew trees dark green, and the urns white. Nevertheless, they are unified because they repeat the same shape. Again, although most of the elements in the set have this shape, they are varied by widely different sizes and positions.

Illus. 6 (page 10) shows a total range of values from the black of the window to the brilliance of the flames. It can be harmonized by confining the hues within a narrow angle of the color circle and giving most of the tones only $\frac{1}{4}$ chroma.

With the exception of some draped sets like Illus. 16 (page 18), few scenes suffer from a lack of variety, but many sets need more unity. Look for elements that can be harmonized. If the values and hues must contrast, introduce unity with shapes and masses as in Illus. 23. When the nature of the scene requires sharp contrasts in line and shape, limit the range of hues, chromas, and values as far as possible (Illus. 81).

Another method of increasing unity is to paint one scene element with hues taken from another. If an inexperienced designer created the set in Illus. 2 (page 7), he would probably make the stones grey, the mortar white, the vines bright green, and the flowers scarlet. The result would seem painfully artificial. It would be much better to work green and red tones into the masonry and show part of the wall overgrown with moss. The mortar should be almost the same tone as the stone so that it is barely visible. Make the vines and flowers as dull as possible without letting them seem either dead or dusty. This treatment would soften the whole effect, make it more pleasing, and much more realistic.

Sharp contrasts and vivid tones are often excellent in costumes. But think twice, or even three times, before you use them in scene designs.

7. PAINTING MODEL SCENERY

Models should be painted either with *show-card colors* or some brand of acrylic paints. Both types are opaque and will hide the brown surface of the carton board.

Show-card colors come in jars, so must be mixed in pans. The tin pans made for baking muffins are ideal as they provide from six to twelve compartments in which you can prepare as many different tones. Dip paint out of the jar with a clean brush and wash the brush thoroughly before dipping it into another color. Using a dirty brush will soon turn your jars of paint to mud.

Acrylics are sold in tubes and must be diluted with water before you mix them. Use white paper as a pallette. Squeeze a little of each color on to the paper and transfer what you need to the mixing pan with a brush. You must still wash your brush each time you use a different color. However, if you become careless, you will spoil only the mixture and not the whole tube.

The pigments in acrylics and show-card colors are not the same as those used for scene paints. Also, cost concerns the scene painter much more than it does the model-maker. For example, when working with real scenery, you can mix permanent red and burnt umber to paint a brick wall. You can get almost the same tone at a fraction of the cost with Venetian red. As your set may need ten or more pounds of paint, the difference is worth considering. A model, on the other hand, requires so little paint that convenience is more important than cost. If you need a brick red and do not have any, it is easier and cheaper to mix bright red and brown than to go out and buy a tube of dull red.

Another important difference is that scene paint is much darker when wet than when dry. Acrylics and show-card colors do not change in this way, but they are shinier and so seem brighter when wet. That has the effect of making them look slightly greyer after they dry.

The instructions which follow refer to the scene-painter's pigments shown in Illus. 85 and Illus. 86. Learn to think in terms of scene-painter's pigments. If you use liberal amounts of emerald green and magenta when designing scenery for a school play, your model will create a false impression: Scene paints of these colors are so costly that few amateur groups would want to squander more than a pound or two of them for any one scene.

When you select your paints, try to match those shown on the color wheel as closely as you can. The following list may be helpful.

White (Whiting)
Buttercup yellow (Chrome yellow medium)
Mustard yellow (French yellow ochre)
Rich, dark, reddish brown (Burnt umber)
Bright red (Permanent red)
Dull brick red (Venetian red)
Deep blue (Ultramarine)
Bright green (Chrome green medium)
Black (Drop black)

Mixing Paint

The color wheel and value chart in Illus. 85 and Illus. 86 are the keys to mixing paint. If you draw a straight line between two pigments on the color wheel, any mixture of those pigments will lie somewhere along that line. Thus, if you mix equal parts of chrome yellow medium and permanent red, you will get orange at a little less than $\frac{1}{2}$ chroma.

You can draw similar lines on the value chart. Mixing equal parts of chrome yellow medium and permanent red will make an orange that is just below "low light" in value.

This does not work perfectly because no pigment is pure. Nevertheless, with a little practice, you will be able to predict the result of any mixture with surprising accuracy.

What do we do if we want our orange to be "light" in value? Using more chrome yellow medium and less permanent red would yield yellow-orange, not true orange. Even that would be well below "light." The answer is to mix yellow and red to get orange and then lighten this with whiting.

Unfortunately, every additional pigment tends to lower the chroma. If the orange is $\frac{1}{2}$ chroma at "low light," adding enough whiting to make it "light" will decrease the chroma to $\frac{1}{4}$.

You can avoid this effect to some extent by a process known to scene painters as SPATTER. This works on the same principle as the colored illustrations in magazines. The tones are applied in small dots. However, playgoers view them from so far away that the individual spots of paint are invisible and blend into a uniform tone. Successive spatters of yellow, red, and white will not create an orange of maximum chroma at "light," but the effect will be much more brilliant than if we mixed the pigments in a pail and simply brushed them on the set.

For models, spray paint from a FIXATIF ATOMIZER instead of spattering it (Illus. 90). The results are the same except that the dots are much smaller. Atomizers made by Grumbacher are available at many art stores.

An atomizer sprays paint from a small bottle. Each tone requires a separate bottle, and each bottle must be washed carefully whenever you use it for a different tone. When you want a more vivid orange than you can get by spattering, the only solution is to buy a more brilliant orange pigment such as *golden ochre* or *milori yellow medium*.

I have mentioned special pigments in order to cover the whole subject of color mixing, but we rarely have need for them. Brightly colored sets take attention from the actors. Hence, most scenes range between neutral grey and $\frac{1}{2}$ chroma. Within this range, our stock pigments will usually suffice. Although my productions have used over two hundred sets, less than five of them called for special paint.

Now, let us suppose that you want to paint something a dark olive green with the pigments shown in Illus. 85 and 86 (page 64). The first step is to locate the desired tone on the charts. Olive green is a slightly yellow green at something less than $\frac{1}{2}$ chroma. We need this at "dark." The nearest pigment is chrome green medium. That is a little on the blue side of true green, a trifle over $\frac{3}{4}$ chroma, and just above "medium" in value. We want to make it yellower, greyer and darker. The chart shows that burnt umber has most of these qualities. A line between it and chrome green medium will cross the

Illus. 90. ATOMIZER. Use one of these to apply spatter coats of paint.

$\frac{1}{2}$ chroma circle just on the yellow side of true green. The burnt umber will also lower the value of the chrome green medium.

Therefore, start with the chrome green medium and add burnt umber a little at a time until you get a tone near the desired chroma. This will probably be too green, so give it a yellowish cast by adding a touch of yellow ochre. The result will have more life if you apply spatter coats of the raw pigments instead of mixing them first and then brushing them on.

A need for olive green at "low dark" brings up another problem. If whiting raises a tone in value, black should darken it. Unfortunately, this does not work. Whiting decreases the chroma but has no effect on the hue. Black, on the other hand, turns almost every mixture into a greyish mud. Hence, you should never mix black with colored pigments. However, when a tone is already as dark as you can get it by other means, you may be able to darken it still further by spattering it *lightly* with black. This is not recommended, but in some cases it may be your only resort.

There is no way to darken a tone without making it duller. If you want a rich dark green, you will need to buy a special pigment such as *malachite green*.

Colored Light

Most sets are, or should be, lit with colored light. The color is produced by shining white lights from electric bulbs through screens known as COLOR MEDIUMS. These are really color filters which strain out all unwanted hues. In this case, the term "medium" does not mean "halfway between light and dark" or "halfway between red and yellow." Think of it simply as the name that stage electricians use for their color filters.

To some extent, the color wheel will help us to predict what effect a colored light will have on our paint. Yellow light makes red paint look somewhat orange, and blue light gives it a violet cast.

Unfortunately, such results are only approximate, and you can sometimes get unpleasant surprises. This is partly due to the fact that the dyes used in these mediums are extremely impure. However, there is a theoretical difference between paint and light that no one seems to understand.

Pale pink lights and pinkish ambers behave about the way the color wheel would lead us to expect. In most cases, they also make scenery much more attractive. Blues, on the other hand, have a curious tendency to bring out any red in a pigment. Make-up often becomes garish under any blue light, and even dark browns may suddenly turn blood red.

The stronger the color, the more apt it is to play unwelcome tricks.

In any event, the effects of colored light can be learned only by experience. You cannot light your models like real sets, but you can try them under different mediums. Get any lamp with a shade that confines the light to one direction. Place your model in a dark room and throw light on it from your lamp. Hold various mediums in front of the lamp and observe what happens to the tones of your model.

Applying Paint

Display models of the type in Illus. 47 (page 37) are painted like ordinary water-color or tempera pictures. On the other hand, a working model should be colored, as far as possible, with the special techniques used by scene painters. This will not only familiarize you with the methods used on a full-scale set but will let you experiment with the actual tones that will be used when the real set is painted.

Base Coat. Scene painting normally begins by covering the entire surface with a BASE COAT. This is brushed on like so much whitewash.

Both carton board and chipboard warp if painted with a brush. You can avoid this by first painting them on the back with plain water and then *immediately* brushing your base coat on to the face.

Spatter Coats. A model with plain walls needs a base coat and two spatter coats. Each spatter coat covers only from one-third to one-half of the surface, so that the coat or coats below it can be seen between the dots of paint. The idea is to cover the wall with three different tones which will blend at a distance to create the desired tone. The combination is much more alive than a flat coat would be. It also camouflages hinges, strippers, and minor defects in the scenery.

Apply the spatter coats with your atomizer. This is messy unless you have a PAINT HOOD. You can make one from a large carton. It should look like the model stage in Illus. 11 (page 15). However, leave it open in front, and cover the top. If you place your model flats in the hood before you spray them, the hood will catch nearly all the stray paint.

Texture. When tones of the base coat and the two spatter coats are close together on the color wheel and value chart, the wall will look almost smooth. If the three tones are fairly far apart, the wall will seem to have TEXTURE.

For example, suppose you want a smooth yellow wall at $\frac{1}{2}$ chroma and "low light" in value. Yellow ochre meets these specifications, but if you merely put on a flat coat of yellow ochre, the result will be hideous. Instead, start with a base coat of yellow ochre slightly darkened and reddened with burnt umber. Our first spatter coat might be yellow ochre with a little whiting and a touch of chrome green medium. The second spatter coat might be yellow ochre given more chroma by adding chrome yellow medium. As all three coats are close to the tone of yellow ochre, the result will appear smooth.

If you want a strong effect of texture, the base coat might be burnt umber with enough whiting to make the mixture "high dark." The first spatter coat could be yellow ochre with enough green to counteract the red of the burnt umber. As the combination of these two coats will be too dark and too low in chroma, our second spatter coat should be chrome yellow medium and white.

Correcting Coats. The second spatter coat rarely creates exactly the desired result. Fortunately, this is not serious. You can make any correction by applying a light spatter coat of the proper tone. If the set looks dingy, go over it with a bright yellow correcting coat. Keep this quite thin, and allow it to dry before judging the effect. If the set is still too dull, add more. In the same way, you can make the set darker or lighter, more yellow, or more green. Experienced painters rarely need more than one correcting coat. However, there is no limit to the number you can use. If you mix too many colors of paint in a pan, the result will be mud—this never happens with spatter coats.

Shadow Coat. No set looks well unless it is heavily shadowed at the top. This concentrates attention on the actors. It also disguises the fact that a 12'-high set is much taller than a real room.

Theoretically, the shadow should be either the base tone at "dark" or "low dark," or a dark value of the tone on the opposite side of the color wheel. For a yellow set, this would mean either dark brown or dark violet at $\frac{1}{2}$ or $\frac{1}{4}$ chroma. However, an equal mixture of burnt umber and ultramarine can be used to shadow almost any set. If the result is not completely satisfactory, it can be corrected by going over the shadow with a thin spatter of whatever tone seems required.

Shadow is applied by spattering. It should normally be so thick at the top of the set that none of the earlier coats show through. For very pale sets, however, it may be wise to leave a little of the undercoats visible.

In any case, the shadow should begin to thin out almost immediately and should fade to nothing at 3' down, so that it blends imperceptively with the tone of the main set. If the set is painted for only one play, bring the shadow down at the corners as I have done in my sketches. For a convertible set, all the shadow should fade out at the same level.

Special Techniques

Most of these require working over a base coat with a brush, sponge, or rag. In such cases, acrylics are much better than show-card colors. When you paint over a show-card color, you may pick up some of the undercoat. This does not happen with acrylics if the first coat is thoroughly dry.

Sponging. The texture created by spattering with widely spaced tones is soft and indefinite. Textures that imitate rough plaster can be created by SPONGING. The chapel in Illus. 18 should be painted in this way. Mix three tones of approximately the same hue. One should be "dark," one "light," and one "high light." Use the "dark" tone for the base coat and apply the others with a fine sponge. Dip the sponge in paint, squeeze it almost dry and pat the paint on the walls.

Different sponges create different textures. Finally, try using a pale tone for the base coat and sponging a darker one over it. The possibilities are

Illus. 91. STENCIL. This is a simplified version of the pattern shown in Illus. 50 (page 38). It is cut from special stencil paper sold by art stores. The cut stencil is then tacked to a frame and held flat against the wall. Paint is then sprayed through it with an atomizer.

endless, and you can have a lot of fun experimenting with them. If the final tone needs correction, you can use spatter. This is quicker and goes on more evenly. It can also be used to soften the texture when the sponged surface seems too rough.

Scumbling. This is similar to sponging. It is done with a rag. Dip the rag in paint, wring it nearly dry and roll it across your flats. Real scenery is usually scumbled with burlap. However, you must use something finer, such as gauze bandage, for your models.

Sponging and scumbling techniques are easy with real sets. Unfortunately, I have not had much luck with them on models built to a scale less than 1"=1'. Pat your sponge or rag on a paper towel until it is nearly dry before applying it to the set. Even so, only the patting and rolling techniques work really well. The dragging procedures that make real scenery look like trowelled plaster, merely make smears on a model. For this effect, get a cheap, $\frac{1}{2}$" varnish brush. Dip it in paint and rub it on a paper towel until it is almost dry. Drag the very tips of the bristles over your flats in short, overlapping sweeps. Do this on the base coat. Then spatter over it until the "trowelling" barely shows. The result is not ideal, but it does suggest the technique that the scene painter should use.

Wallpaper. Simple patterns with straight lines and small spots like those in Illus. 46 and 47 (pages 36, 37) are easy to handle. For a more elaborate pattern try covering your model with self-adhesive plastic sheets. I used this for Illus. 50 (page 38). A real set built from this model would need a greatly simplified design applied with a stencil (Illus. 91).

You can also stencil a pattern on the model. Apply a base coat, lay the stencil in each place where you want your pattern to appear, and spray on the paint. The spray coat should be about as strong as the base coat that shows through it. When the stencilling is complete, add two spatter coats. These will soften the design until it is barely visible, which is the effect you want. The audience should be aware that the pattern exists but should not pay undue attention to it.

Woodwork. Apply a flat base coat of the desired color. Then *grain* the wood as shown in Illus. 92. Use the varnish brush recommended for "trowelling." Study the graining in real wood and try to reproduce the pattern.

Graining should normally be so faint that it is almost invisible from a few feet away. Even so, it makes the woodwork seem much more realistic. Woodwork painted white must be grained in pale blue or violet. This kills the chalky look that flat white paint would create.

Scenery intended to represent rough boards must show cracks. The crack itself should be dark brown. You will also need to paint a line on each side of it. These should be slightly paler than the rest of the wood.

Masonry. When you want to paint convincing stone or brick, the secret lies in getting the mortar lines in the right places and avoiding the faults shown in Illus. 93. Study real stone- or brick-work of the type you want and follow the same pattern in your model. However, some modern masonry has vertical mortar lines that run the whole height of the wall, and some stone buildings are covered with a thin facing that exposes tall narrow stones at the corners (Illus. 95). Such tricks are apt to be unconvincing when the masonry is merely paint on canvas. In fact, if you paint yellow brick walls with long, vertical joints, half your audience will not even realize that they are supposed to represent brick.

Masonry takes more time to paint than a plain wall. However, when it is properly done, even spectators in the front row cannot tell the results from real masonry. No model can be that realistic, but yours can train you for the day when you get a chance to paint a real set.

Painting Brick. For smooth brickwork, paint the wall the color of your bricks (Illus. 93). Rule in the mortar lines. Rule a *fine* shadow line under and on one side of each brick. Spatter the whole lightly with shadow paint.

Illus. 92. GRAINING. Wood grain is imitated with a cheap ½-inch, varnish brush. Apply a base coat the desired tone of the wood. Mix two graining tones, one lighter than the base tone and one darker. Dip your brush in paint, wipe it nearly dry, and apply the grain with the tips of the bristles. The door and frame shown are the type used for working models like Illus. 50 (page 38). They are painted on flat pieces of chipboard and shadowed to indicate thickness.

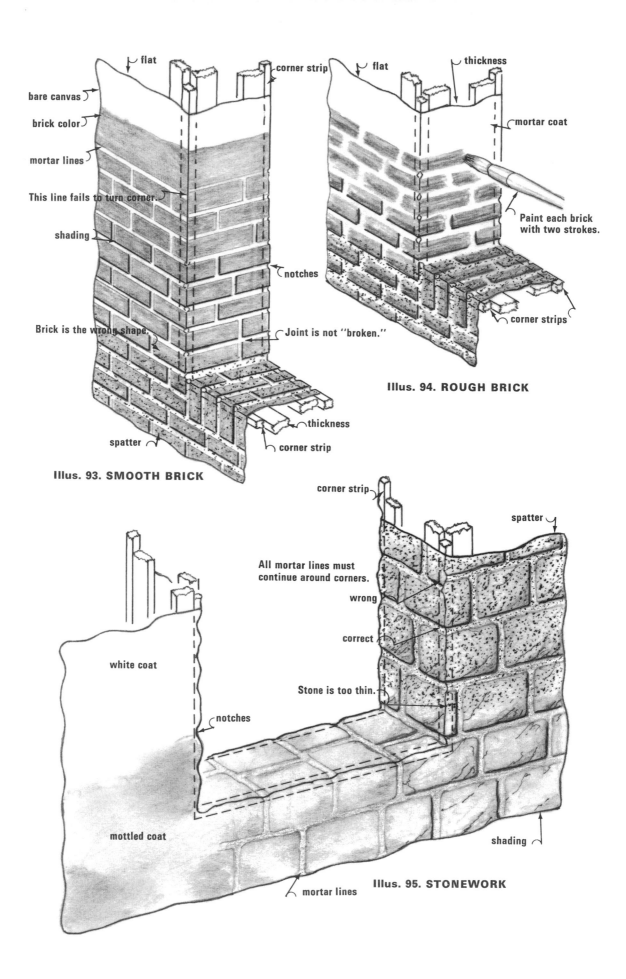

Illus. 93. SMOOTH BRICK

flat

bare canvas

brick color

mortar lines

This line fails to turn corner.

shading

Brick is the wrong shape.

spatter

thickness

corner strip

corner strip

notches

Joint is not "broken."

Illus. 94. ROUGH BRICK

flat

thickness

mortar coat

Paint each brick with two strokes.

corner strips

Illus. 95. STONEWORK

corner strip

spatter

All mortar lines must continue around corners.

wrong

correct

Stone is too thin.

white coat

notches

mottled coat

mortar lines

shading

When you want rough brick, paint the whole wall the tone of the mortar (Illus. 94). Paint each brick separately with two strokes of your brush. This requires a brush with its point cut off square. The remaining tip should be a trifle broader than half the scale height of a brick. If your set is on a scale of $1'' = 1'$, the tip of the brush should be $\frac{1}{8}''$ across. After painting all the bricks, shadow each one. Finish with a light spray of shadow tone.

This procedure works even with bricks that are supposed to be painted white. I once painted a whole exterior set in that way, and the result was completely satisfactory. I made the mortar slightly darker and bluer than the bricks. The shadow tone was grey-blue about one shade darker than the mortar.

Painting Stone. Draw the stones lightly with an *indelible pencil*. This will later bleed through the paint, so that you can see your design even after you have applied several coats.

Cover the whole area with acrylic paint of a neutral tone. Mix three batches of paint nearly the tone you want the stone to be. For the walls in Illus. 2 (page 7) use grey at "light" with a little blue added, red at "low light," and $\frac{1}{4}$ chroma and green at "medium" and $\frac{1}{4}$ chroma. Paint these on the model in patches with a brush and blend them into one another while they are still wet. The result will look like the mottled coat in Illus. 95.

Add a little whiting and a touch of green to the light grey, and paint in the mortar lines with this. Mix burnt umber with ultramarine and draw a shadow line below each stone and on one side. You may also want to paint in a few cracks.

Finally, spray a thin coat of the shadow paint over the whole wall to create a rough texture. You will be amazed to see how much the result resembles real stone.

Foliage. No matter how well you paint foliage borders, they will not look like real trees (Illus. 25 through Illus. 27). The best plan is to make them as unobtrusive as possible. Do not try to represent any particular type of tree. Paint rough ovals by blending several shades of green in the same way you blended the stonework. Then paint individual leaves in batches. Make some darker than the blended areas and others lighter. Have the leaves overhang the blended areas to give them rough outlines. Each leaf should be painted with one stroke of a blunt brush. This will make them almost square. How well it looks will depend on how you arrange the blended patches and the clusters of leaves within them. Illus. 26 (page 25) is an example.

Vines like those in Illus. 2 (page 7) cannot be painted convincingly. Either find artificial vines or omit them. However, artificial vines will be much fuller and will seem more real if you first paint vines on the set and then arrange artificial ones over those you have painted.

The great secret of scene painting is to go ahead and do it, even when you are sure you will fail. Over and over again, I have needed to paint something I never tried before and for which I had no model. At one time or another, I have painted a velvet drapery, a winter landscape, and a pile of straw—with no previous experience whatever. The results were far from masterpieces, but they satisfied my audience. You will never paint anything if you are afraid to try. But if you do try, you will be surprised at how often you succeed.

(Opposite)
Illus. 93-95. These show methods of representing masonry with full-scale scenery. Thickness pieces are essential. However, plain thickness pieces have straight edges that do not resemble masonry. To correct this, we nail square strips at the corners and notch these at the mortar lines. You cannot use strips with a model, but you can notch the back edges of your thickness pieces.

Illus. 96. USING TOUCHES TO LOCATE A SCENE. The basic set in Illus. 73 might represent a hospital, a hotel lobby, or a railway station. I have established this design as a hotel by: (1) adding a potted palm; (2) providing a marble dado; (3) introducing signs that point to special rooms; (4) making the doors on stage left represent an elevator. This last could appear in a hospital but is unlikely in a railway station. A mail rack behind the desk would help to indicate a hotel, but it would be largely hidden by the alcove and would be difficult to build.

8. EXPOSITION

When the curtain rises, the spectators are presented with an unknown world, and they must be told many things before they can understand, let alone enjoy, the play. These needed explanations are called EXPOSITION.

Exposition presents difficult problems. As the characters in the play are already familiar with the facts, they cannot mention them without sounding unnatural. For example, it would be absurd to start a play by having one character announce to another, "As you know, this is the court of Spain in the year 1492. That Genoese adventurer, Christopher Columbus, has been trying for months to ʾave our beloved Queen Isabella fit out a fleet for him.."

In times past, however, playwrights *were* often that obvious. Modern authors rarely indulge in open exposition, but they need all the help they can get from the designer. He is in an excellent position to give it, because he can convey information both subtly and instantly. Thus, an audience seeing the set in Illus. 13 (page 17) can tell at a glance that the scene is laid in the living room of a wealthy home. Similarly, Illus. 2 (page 7) represents a castle and Illus. 18 (page 20) a Spanish mission.

The set in Illus. 73 (page 54) is less informative. It is obviously a lobby or something of the sort, but it could represent a hotel, a hospital, or a railway station. Here, the costume designer can help. A bell-hop shows that the room is in a hotel; a nurse, or an intern in a white coat with a stethoscope in his pocket, will indicate a hospital; and a redcap tells the spectators that they are in a railroad station.

Although the costume designer can do part of your work for you, you should not depend on him. The sketch in Illus. 96 shows how to make the plan in Illus. 73 represent a hotel lobby. Try to think of ways to make the same basic set let the audience know that it is a hospital, or a station.

Conveying information in this way is an important part of the designer's job. He should do all he can to tell the audience as much as possible. The stage directions usually list the more important items, but the set can often go much further.

For example, suppose you read a play and discover that the first scene is laid in the office of a man named Ames, Sales Manager for the Britt Manufacturing Corporation. This is a comparatively small firm. It is a Friday afternoon in mid-October. Ames is badly overworked. Business has been poor, and there has just been a meeting at which he has tried to get more action out of his sales force. How much of this could you tell the audience with your set if there is no one on stage when the scene opens?

Illus. 97 proves that the design can convey all of it except the nature of the meeting. A full-scale set would reveal several points not mentioned in the caption. The furniture is shabby and old-fashioned, confirming the fact that the firm is small and not prosperous. Ames' desk holds three telephones—an indication that he is busy. There is also a photograph of a woman, presumably his wife. The disarranged chairs can be seen more clearly in the floor plan (Illus. 76, page 56). Their positions are evidence of a recent meeting. Otherwise, they would have been placed in neat rows. The only bit of exposition that the set does not handle is the fact that it was a sales meeting. The people present might have been directors of the company or department heads.

Touches

Devices for conveying information are called TOUCHES. Generally speaking, touches enrich a play, and the more you can add, the better. A touch can be too obvious, that is, when it seems forced and unnatural. Any item that might reasonably be present in real life will be accepted by the audience.

Touches are inherently more subtle than spoken words. Ames *might* say, "Friday has certainly been my unlucky day," or, "October has been a tough month." However, he is unlikely to make either statement, and it is hard to believe that he would make two such remarks in the first minute or two after the curtain opens. However, the touches of the calendar and the chart convey both facts and do it in a completely plausible way.

What if the playwright explains some of these points in his lines? Should the designer repeat the same information? The answer is a decided, "Yes!" A spectator may want a fact before the lines can provide it. He may miss a line—especially in an opening scene, or he may ignore a point because he does not realize that it will be important later, and forget it before it becomes important. A designer's touch generally remains in plain sight. Each spectator can observe the various touches in any order he chooses, and he can refer to one whenever he feels the need. Also, a much stronger impression is conveyed through several mediums than by words alone.

When a playwright makes the same point twice, playgoers who caught it the first time are bored by the repetition. This is never true when an idea is repeated in different ways. I always try to direct a play so that a totally deaf person could follow the action. I like my actors to use inflections that would reveal their moods to a foreigner who speaks no English. Scene designs, costume designs, light, and sound should work towards the same end. No one but the playwright can tell the whole story, but the more the rest of us reinforce his words, the better the production will be.

Basic Facts

Place and time are the designer's chief responsibilities and also his greatest opportunities.

Place. It is not enough for a set to indicate a living room, a kitchen, or an office—often you can tell the audience *where* it is: what country, what part of the country, whether it is a town house, an apartment, a farm, or a hunting lodge. Is it new or old, well kept or shabby?

What kind of people own it? What sort are we likely to meet there? Are they rich or poor, educated or ignorant, simple or pretentious? Although the sets in Illus. 30 (page 27), 47 (page 37), 50 (page 38), and 84 (page 63) all have the same floor plan, they suit different types of plays and represent homes belonging to different types of people. Study each one and try to make up your mind what the owners are like. Would you expect them to be sophisticated or stodgy, gay or gloomy, stiff or friendly? Do the same thing with all the other sets in this book. The more practice you have in interpreting the sets of other designers, the more you will be able to make your own sets convey information about the play and the characters.

Ask yourself every question you can about the place and the people. Be as specific as possible. In most cases, the answers are obvious. The problem is to find enough questions.

When you ask yourself questions, try to be as detailed and definite as you can. However, the answers you may find should sometimes be deliberately indefinite. For instance, many plays deal with "an average American family." Even if you could find a way to show that the scene is located at 3207 Hudson Street in New Haven, you should *not* use it. You would even be wrong to indicate whether the scene is laid in Connecticut, Alabama, or Oregon. You need to suggest that the action might occur in *any* American home. If you place the scene in a specific section of the country, your audience may think it is typical of that section and does not represent Americans in general.

At first, it may seem difficult to decide just how definite you should be. Actually, it is easy—if a piece of information will help the spectators understand the play, and if you can convey this information by your design, you should certainly do so. On the other hand, when a fact about the setting or the characters will not make the action clearer, you should avoid any attempt to bring it to the attention of your audience.

Time. Writers of historical novels often fill several pages before telling their readers whether the action takes place in 1580 or 1850. This will not do in the theatre. An audience should be able to identify the period as soon as the curtain rises. Costumes do more to specify a period than scenery does, but this does not relieve the scene designer of his responsibility for fixing the date when he can.

If a play is laid before 1900, and the action is not connected with any specific historical event, such as Caesar's assassination or the American Civil War, it may be better to keep the date indefinite. Thus, *Romeo and Juliet* is a universal love story. The more general it seems, the better. The action indicates Renaissance Italy, but that covers the whole period from 1275 to 1600. To be more precise would weaken the play's universal quality. The costumes must conform to the same general period, but the scene designer can, and should, be less specific.

On the other hand, scenery for a play laid during the American Revolution should fix the date as accurately as possible. A playgoer familiar with the history of the war may be interested in whether the action begins in 1776 or in 1780. Sometimes even a day or two may make a difference. Characters in a Revolutionary play act in one way before the battle of Trenton and in an entirely different way after Washington's victory.

Similar problems arise in modern plays. If the plot deals with the Great Depression, try to indicate a date in the 1930's. Even when the year is not important, the season may be—or the time of month, day of the week, or hour of the day. Flowers can indicate the season (jonquils for spring, chrysanthemums for fall). Illus. 97 uses a calendar to indicate both the time of the month and the day of the week. Lighting can show day or night. When you need to be more specific, use a clock. However, try to find a more subtle touch if you can. Thus, a Sunday paper, complete with colored comics, scattered about a living room tells the audience that the time is late Sunday morning.

Openings. Doors and other openings through which actors enter and exit, are important sources of information. The whole meaning of a scene may depend on whether a character comes from the library or the kitchen. Whenever possible, each door should lead to a specific place. This raises problems.

In most sets, wall space is at a premium. Furniture cannot be in front of a door, and it is almost always a mistake to put any furniture downstage of a door in the back wall. However, furniture may be moved downstage of a door that is not used while the furniture is in place. The hutch table in Illus. 6 (page 10), for example, could be moved away from the wall. Its top could be lowered and chairs set around it in preparation for a meal, which is fine if no one enters or exits through the Dutch door during the time that the table is in this position.

Finding room for one or two doors in a set is usually easy, but a third door often causes difficulty. If you need *more* than three doors, the difficulty becomes serious. Illus. 7 (page 12) shows one solution. The main set has only two doors. However, the one in the back wall leads to three different places. A character coming along the hall from stage left arrives from outside. The hall to stage right leads to the dining room and kitchen. The stairs serve the bedrooms. If the center doorway were a broad arch, you could introduce another entrance by putting a door in the backing and adding a second backing behind it.

Stairs can raise the level of an opening, permitting you to put furniture in front of it (Illus. 79, page 57). This plan also shows a door in a jog—this occupies a minimum of the floor space that could be used for other purposes. As the areas downstage of this door must be kept clear of furniture anyway, you can locate a door beside it without complicating your problem. Illus. 81 (page 58) shows no less than seven entrances! The whole design had to be arranged to make these seven openings possible.

Characters. We can also add touches to convey information about the people who inhabit a place. Thus, if the Sales Manager in Illus. 97 keeps a large picture of his wife on his desk, it tells the audience something about him. If his secretary has a rose in a glass on her desk, it gives a clue to the sort of person she is.

Even a hotel bedroom can provide character touches. Illus. 21 (page 22) shows a room in a cheap hotel, where no one would care to stay unless he were hard up. Introduce a battered suitcase with several stickers on it, and the audience knows that the occupant has travelled a good deal. An almost empty whisky bottle standing beside a water glass on the table would add still more information.

Touches in a play are more significant than they would be in real life. While a man may have whisky in his hotel room without being a drunkard, a bottle that appears on a set leaves no doubt at all.

Symbols

When you can *symbolize* an idea, it usually pays to do so. For instance, it would be hard for an actress to let the audience know that she is thinking about her sweetheart in the navy. But if the set contains a model of his ship, every time she glances towards it she announces that she is thinking of her lover.

Symbols can be effective even when they are extremely subtle. In one play, a character decided to live a completely free life. However, as the action progressed, he found himself more and more hemmed in by conventions and responsibilities. In the end, he realized that he had almost no freedom at all. The designer symbolized this by putting as many doors and windows in the set as he could. One by one these were shut. The last, and most prominent, door was closed with a bang just after the climax of the play. It was not apparent from the beginning that the doors and windows were used as symbols, but everyone subconsciously felt that the leading character's freedom was being progressively cut off.

A somewhat similar device can become a symbol for the set in Illus. 6 (page 10). The characters in a melodrama are often menaced by some unknown terror. If they believe that the menace is already inside the house, the door in the back wall should be closed to shut the characters in with the terror. However, if the menace is expected to come from outside, the door should be left open just enough to

Illus. 97. DESIGNING TO CONVEY ADDITIONAL INFORMATION. This does much more than tell the audience that it represents an office. The lettering on the window gives the name of the firm. The door indicates that the room is occupied by a man named Ames, and that he is Sales Manager. Note that this requires swinging the door onstage instead of offstage as shown in the plan (Illus. 76, page 56). The calendar fixes the date as a Friday in October, and the clock gives the hour as 4:05. This must be in afternoon because it is daylight outside. The company must be small and poor, or Ames would not need to share his office with his secretary and a conference table. The line on the chart shows that sales have slumped. The disarranged chairs announce that there has recently been a meeting of some sort.

show the darkness outside. This will then act as a symbol of the menace itself.

Modern artists often use abstract or distorted forms as symbols. Thus, a painted eye may suggest watchfulness, or a jagged shape may indicate harshness or pain. Attempts to do this sort of thing in the theatre have usually failed. Audiences tend to find abstract forms funny and joke about them. Keep your symbols realistic. Anyone who understands the symbol will appreciate it.

Abstract Design Elements. The design elements described in Chapter 5 act as subconscious symbols. When used correctly, they strengthen the emotional impact of the play. Carelessly introducing the wrong symbols weakens the mood and may even destroy it.

Lines. Straight lines are direct and definite. Smooth, irregular curves that just miss being straight suggest serenity. The adobe chapel in Illus. 18 (page 20) shows two sets of contrasting lines. Those of the walls curve gently, while those of the pews are harsh and angular. Although this is strictly realistic, it symbolizes perfectly the sharp contrast between the physical hardships that the missionaries endure and the spiritual peace that they enjoy. Deep curves, like those in Illus. 23 (page 23) imply richness and luxury. Small, fussy curves are usually undesirable unless they are so broken that the eye is not tempted to follow them. This is the case in Illus. 2, where the fussiness of the vines is needed to keep the scene from being dominated by the strong sweeps of the walls.

The directions of the lines are extremely important. When horizontals dominate, the effect is calm and restrained.

Dominant verticals suggest aspiration and lofty ideals. Amateur stages are rarely high enough to permit tall verticals, but Illus. 25 (page 24) may give some idea of the effect that verticals can produce. Also, note how the winding stair in Illus. 81 (page 58) creates an effect of height.

Diagonals are dynamic. They imply action. This is one reason why it often pays to rake a set. However, do not get the idea that you can make a talky play more interesting by placing the set at an angle. The set must always harmonize with the play.

Stairs, especially those with handrails, also introduce diagonals and give actors more opportunities to move along diagonal lines. When diagonals conflict strongly, they suggest violent disputes or even actual combats. Unfortunately, it is hard to introduce *conflicting* diagonals unless you have room for

two flights of stairs—one slanting to the right and one to the left.

Most lines in a set are the outlines of real objects, such as doors and sofas. The designer can control these by choosing objects with the sort of outlines he needs. Thus, in Illus. 30 (page 27), the straight, hard lines emphasize the horizontal and create a static effect. Introducing diagonals makes the set gayer and more dynamic (Illus. 47, page 37). Illus. 84 (page 63) replaces most of the straight lines with gentle curves. Illus. 50 (page 38) softens the lines by making the furniture blend with the walls.

Shapes. Abstract shapes rarely have much importance in scene design, but occasions arise when they can be highly effective (Illus. 18, page 20). Again, the fact that the trees in Illus. 25 form shapes like Gothic arches suggests that the forest is a natural cathedral, and creates a religious atmosphere for the play.

Masses. These have as much effect on the atmosphere of a play as they do on the balance of a stage picture. Everyone feels that tragedies and melodramas are "heavy" and that farces are "light." Hence, a set for a tragedy should seem more massive than one for a farce.

The effect of greater mass can sometimes be achieved by using broader thickness pieces to suggest thicker walls. Steps and platforms also add weight. Illus. 25 would seem much lighter if the whole set were on the same level. Usually, however, you must depend on the fact that darkness suggests mass. Sets for comedies are normally painted in tones above "low light." Those for tragedies rarely rise above "high dark."

The strength of the light has even more effect than the value of the paint. It would be almost impossible to play a tragedy on a brightly lit stage, but most comedies can use all the light you can give them. Comedy melodramas should be lit dimly because they are based on the contrast between the eerie atmosphere and the absurd situations.

Although interest adds mass when we are dealing with balance, this is not true from the standpoint of symbolism. The simpler a set is, the more massive it seems. Adding pictures or small props will make it seem lighter, not heavier.

Tones. Colors above "medium" in value and strong in chroma suggest gaiety and are therefore suitable to comedies. However, they should be used for costumes and small props rather than for the walls of a set. Dark and greyed tones do well for tragedy and serious drama. They can be effectively used for walls and large pieces of furniture. Tones on the left of the color wheel (Illus. 85, page 64) seem warm. Those on the right seem cool and also appear to recede.

These facts are important, but the idea of warm and cool tones can be misleading. For several years, I believed that a set for a warm, friendly play should be painted in warm colors. The result was usually a dingy brown. I have used red sets and yellow sets successfully but neither hue gave a warm effect. The red sets were either dramatic or theatrical; the yellow ones seemed frivolous. When you want to create an atmosphere of warmth, you will do better to paint your walls soft greens or blues and then add warm tones in the draperies, upholstery, and costumes. Small, bright patches of red, orange, or yellow help. These can be added by props, such as vases, flowers, candles, or books.

Conventional color symbols are not much use to scene designers. Hues symbolize different things when used in different ways. Green stands for springtime, youth, safety, jealousy, and ghosts. Red suggests fire, blood, and danger. Red and green together conjure up Christmas.

Nevertheless, some tones seem particularly suited to certain plays. Others are flatly inappropriate. When I studied design, we were told to sketch a set using only one hue and make it darker or lighter to bring out the details. Although we had a free choice, all of us used dull blue-green except one girl—and she used blue-grey. In this case, the play had a strong and obvious mood. I feel certain that scenery painted in warm or bright tones would have ruined that play. Other plays would have permitted a wider range of choice.

I have produced the same play once with a brown set and once with a blue set, and both were equally effective. Nevertheless, you should always ask yourself what tone or tones will best fit the scene for which your set is intended. If you do, you are not apt to go far wrong.

9. ARENA DESIGN

Any large, flat area, such as a gymnasium, a ballroom, or even a tennis court, can be turned into a stage for arena production by arranging one or two rows of seats around a playing space. The total area must be at least 25′ × 30′, but there is no other essential requirement.

The seats may be merely chairs placed on the level of the stage. This permits only two rows and limits the audience to about a hundred people. Also, the view from the second row is far from ideal. These difficulties can be overcome by building portable platforms on which the seats are arranged in tiers. Raising the seats provides excellent sight-lines and makes it possible to include as many rows as the size of the auditorium will permit.

A number of groups own permanent arena theatres. Most of these have fixed banks of seats, and some have elaborate gridirons and lighting equipment. A few are large enough to hold seven or eight hundred spectators.

Seating Plans

Although a permanent seating arrangement has important advantages, it also has one serious drawback. Entrances and exits must be made by the aisles. If these are fixed, the designer is severely hampered.

Illus. 98 through Illus. 101 show possible plans when the playing space is rectangular. Each of these is desirable for some scenes and a nuisance for others. Thus, the corner aisles in Illus. 101 work well for exteriors and for most plays by Shakespeare. However, they make realistic interiors impossible; no normal room has doors in the corners (Illus. 102). With makeshift seating, the designer can place the aisles to suit his sets. The only limitation is that he cannot move the aisles when he designs two or more sets for the same play.

Permanent arenas have been built in round, oval

and horseshoe shapes. The number of aisles varies from three to six.

Arena Geography

As an arena has neither up- nor down-stage and no right or left, we must use a different scheme for providing directions. Although there is no universal agreement on the best method, the clock system shown in Illus. 101 is convenient and accurate. Also, actors find it easy to learn because the clock principle is used by aviators—and war films have made it familiar to everyone.

Set Design

As arena stages have no walls, plays can often be produced without any scenery. When scene units are used, they are normally restricted to low platforms. However, when a permanent auditorium has a gridiron, symbolic forms can be hung from it.

The fact that scenery is unnecessary may seem to eliminate the designer's problems or at least simplify them. Actually, they are made more difficult. The arena designer must make furniture and other props serve all the functions that the proscenium designer provides with scenery.

Wall Lines. Advocates of arena staging claim that the impact of a production is increased by the fact that playgoers are forced to exercise their imaginations. This may be true, but nothing is gained by straining the spectators' powers of imagination. There is even less excuse for asking an audience to mentally reconstruct the set and visualize an impossible furniture plan as one that might exist in an actual room. Nevertheless, many arena designers are content to place clumps of furniture in any convenient areas. They then expect the audience to view the action in such an arrangement as something that might take place in real life. Although audiences have demonstrated an incredible capacity to overlook completely unrealistic conventions in

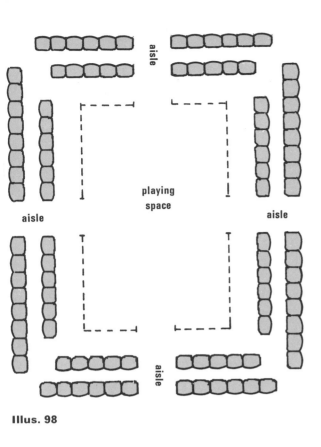

Illus. 98

SEATING PLANS. As the locations of the aisles control the positions of the entrances, they also control the design of the set.

Illus. 99

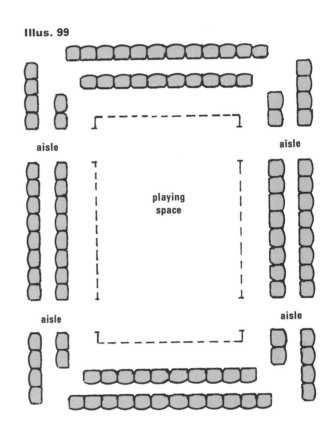

Illus. 100

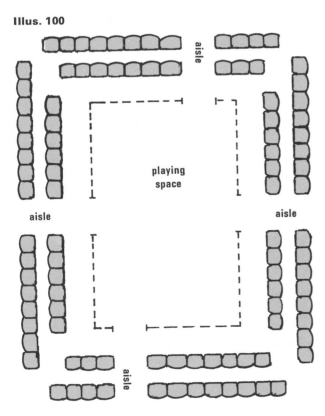

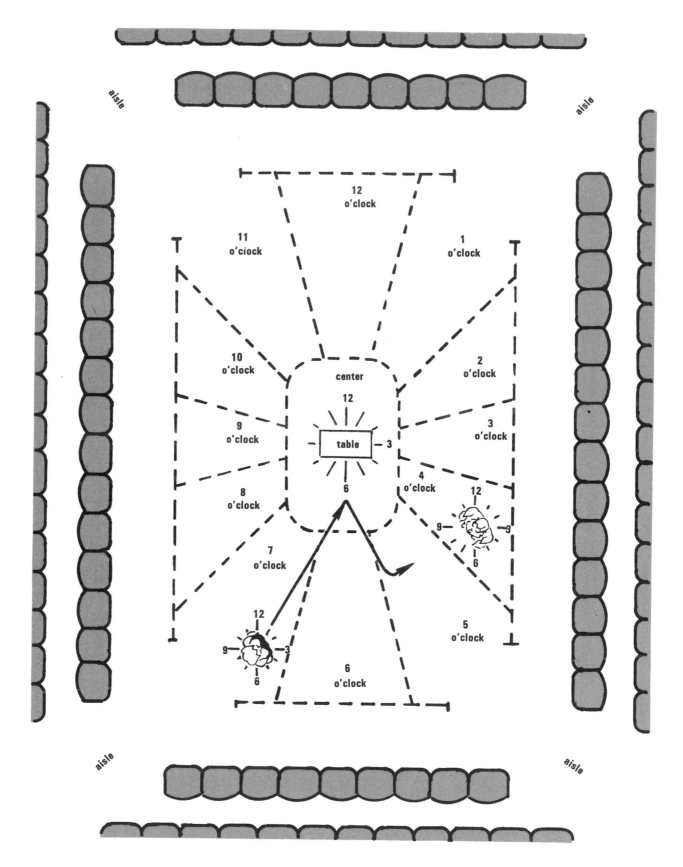

Illus. 101. ARENA GEOGRAPHY. Directions are designated like the hours on a clock. Let one end of the stage arbitrarily represent 12 o'clock and number the other directions and areas accordingly. Each performer and each large prop has a separate clock. Thus, the diagram shows a girl at 7 o'clock. She will move 1 o'clock to a position that is 6 o'clock from the table, center. She then moves 5 o'clock and turns 2 o'clock to face the man at 4 o'clock.

arena productions, it is certainly the designer's duty to restrict these to an absolute minimum.

For this reason, I advocate starting a design by drawing imaginary wall lines and then arranging furniture to match. Even if this does not relieve the audience from the need to perform mental gymnastics, it lets the director and actors think in terms of plausible actions in a believable room.

A set becomes easier to visualize when the wall lines are stressed by placing furniture along them. All the sets in Illus. 102 through Illus. 107 do this.

Try to locate at least one important piece of furniture against each wall and one in or near each corner. Unless this is done, actors will have no excuse to approach the empty wall or corner. That makes it difficult for the director to plan his movements and groupings.

Sightlines. When a short woman is seated, her eyes are about 3' 9" above the floor. If the first row of seats is on the stage level, no bulky prop can safely be higher than 3' 6". Tall, thin props, such as candles or pens in a desk set, give no trouble. We can even build a summerhouse by making a lattice of thin strips. However, chairs with high backs are useless, and such items as screens and chiffoniers are out of the question. Even a 3' 6" bar is undesirable

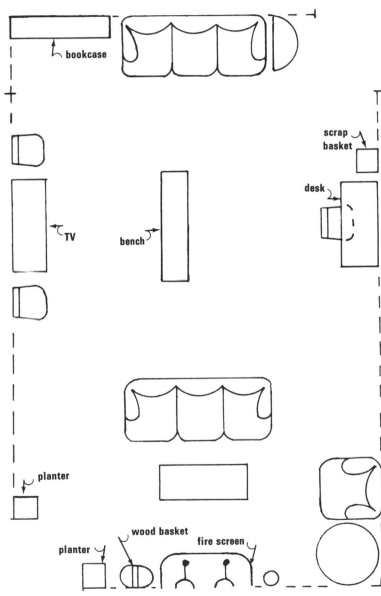

Illus. 102. ENTRANCES AT CORNERS. This is an arena version of the set in Illus. 30 (page 27) made to fit the seating plan in Illus. 101. As that places the doors in the corners, the effect is unrealistic.

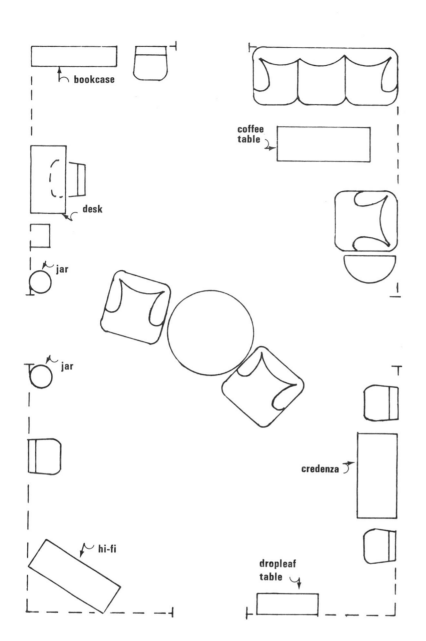

bookcase

coffee table

desk

jar

jar

credenza

hi-fi

dropleaf table

Illus. 103. ENTRANCES CENTERED. The seating plan in Illus. 98 controlled this version of the set in Illus. 72 (page 54). It is weak because the four doors left little scope for a more satisfactory arrangement.

because some spectators will have to watch the action over it.

Unfortunately, some plays cannot be staged without one or two high props or scene units. In many of them, pianos are required by the action. *Arsenic and Old Lace* needs a long stairway. *Romeo and Juliet* is unthinkable without a balcony. In cases of this sort, the only solution is to place such awkward features in one or two aisles.

These may be used as part of the set when the action demands them. Nevertheless, they introduce a completely unrealistic convention which should be avoided if possible. Compare this with the situation on a proscenium stage where stairs are highly desirable.

When the seats are arranged in tiers, the height of the first row can be added to 3′ 6″, and the result fixes the sightlines. Thus, if the first row is 1′ above the stage floor, props 4′ 6″ may be used. This permits the use of bars, sideboards, and chairs with high backs.

Axis of Movement. Many plays revolve around two opposing forces that can be symbolized by doors or props. Thus, a play may deal with someone who must decide between facing danger or hardship for some important cause or retiring to comfortable obscurity. One door can lead to action and the other to safety. The actor will be able to symbolize how his character feels at each moment by moving towards one door or the other.

The altar in Illus. 18 (page 20) is a prop that

could also be used in this way. If a character is torn between a desire to serve God and a longing for worldly pleasures, this could be symbolized by the actor's movements between the altar and the door.

Such symbols establish an AXIS OF MOVEMENT. In a proscenium set, the symbols must not be close together, but their exact locations are rarely crucial. Arena designs are a different matter. Many directors like to establish an axis of movement whenever the play permits. They then plan the whole action around this. In such cases, the designer should place the key doors or props at opposite corners (Illus. 102 and Illus. 104) or at opposite ends (Illus. 103) of the set.

He should also try to provide a clear path for the axis of movement. Illus. 102 through Illus. 104 all fall short here. An actor moving from one door to the other would have to follow an irregular curve. This would obscure the axis to a point where it would make little or no impression on the audience. In Illus. 105, on the other hand, the axis of movement is a smooth, symmetrical curve. For most plays, this is better than a straight axis as it leads to more graceful movements.

Variety. Proscenium designers have no difficulty providing variety. Illus. 30, 47, 50 and 84 all have the same floor plan. However, the wall treatments are so different that a group could use two of these

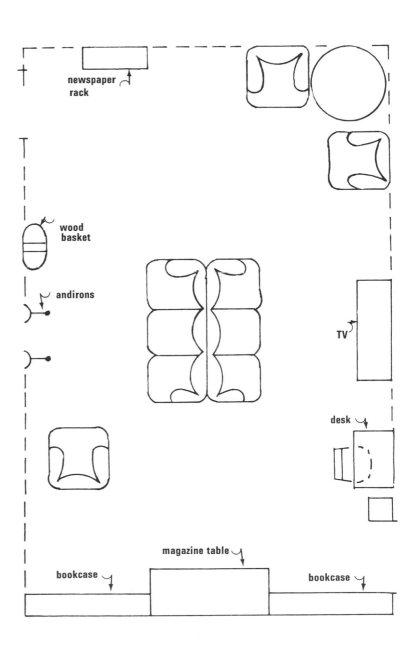

Illus. 104. DOORS NEAR ENDS. The plan in Illus. 99 makes design fairly easy. Its chief fault is that it does not permit raked sets. The parallel set shown is an arena version of the club room in Illus. 78 (page 57).

newspaper rack

wood basket

andirons

TV

desk

magazine table

bookcase

bookcase

sets in the same season without having the duplication noticed by the audience.

Arena living rooms, on the other hand, all have a strong family resemblance. I have tried to vary the plans in Illus. 102 through Illus. 105 as much as possible, but I suspect that few playgoers would be aware of the differences between them. If you design three or more living-room sets for the same season, variety becomes a major consideration.

Try to choose furniture of different styles, weights, and colors. Thus, the sofas in Illus. 50, 78 and 84 would be obviously different even if they were used

Illus. 105. DOORS OFF CENTER. The unsymmetrical seating plan in Illus. 100 has definite advantages. It tends to create interesting furniture arrangements. Also, it offers chances to provide a strong diagonal axis of movement and hence has somewhat the effect of a raked set. The set shown here was based on that in Illus. 13 (page 17), but I have added two doors to create an axis of movement.

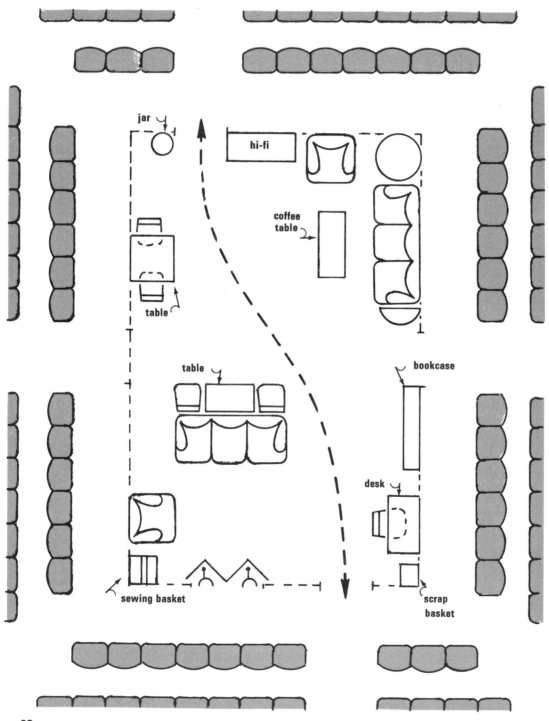

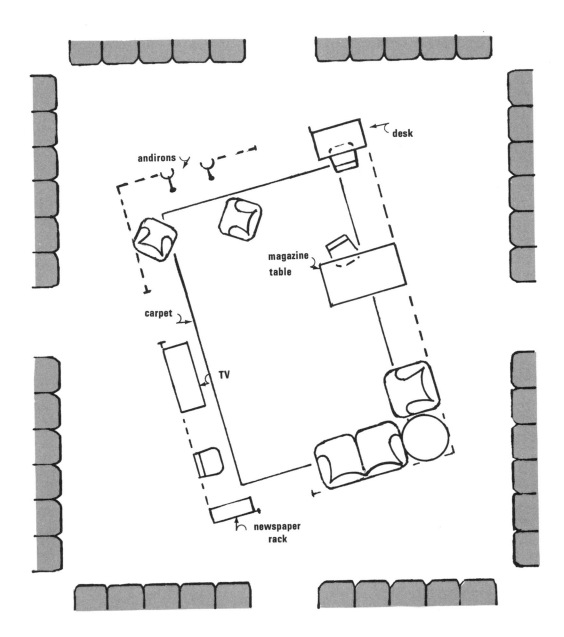

Illus. 106. RAKED SET. This is another version of the club room set in Illus. 78 (page 57) and 104. Note that changing the angle of the set involved a drastic rearrangement of the furniture. A raked set takes up more than its parallel counterpart even though the actual playing space is smaller. This creates problems when the auditorium is cramped. With a large auditorium, however, the seating plan for a raked set provides more chairs in each row. Note that the arena for a raked set must be more nearly square than those in Illus. 98 through Illus. 105.

in arena sets with the same floor plan. Slipcovers are valuable here. Use plain material for one set, small patterns for the next, and bold prints for the third. Nevertheless, you cannot afford to sacrifice appropriateness for variety. If you need dark, plain upholstery in your first set and your second must represent a club room like that in Illus. 78, you cannot introduce gay, pink and yellow slipcovers merely to be different.

Raked Sets. Designers who arrange furniture in random groups have no use for raked sets. However, anyone who has learned the value of axes will find that raking an arena set has important advantages when the nature of the play permits. Illus. 106 shows a raked version of the set in Illus. 104. We cannot say that it is better without knowing the play for which it was designed. However, it is certainly more interesting and dynamic. It would also provide the director with a wider variety of expressive movements and groupings.

Furthermore, a raked set permits the use of jogs and alcoves (Illus. 10). This helps the designer to

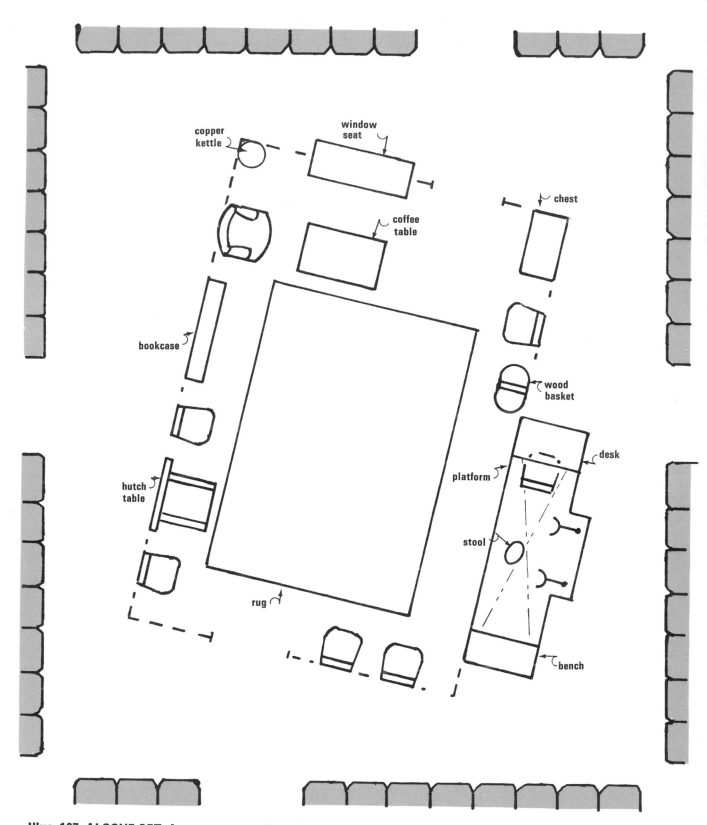

Illus. 107. ALCOVE SET. An arrangement like this creates an interesting floor plan and also makes a set seem less formal. This one is an arena version of the set in Illus. 5 (page 9) and Illus. 6 (page 10). It could also be worked with the seating plan in Illus. 98, but not with those in Illus. 99 or 101.

achieve both variety and interest. Theoretically, jogs and alcoves can be used when the set is placed parallel, but this seldom works well in practice.

As Illus. 106 and Illus. 107 show, a raked set calls for an arena that is more nearly square than one where the set is placed parallel. Also, either the set must be smaller or the arena must be larger. When these conditions are undesirable or impossible, we can get a raked effect by placing the entrances (and the aisles) off center (Illus. 105). However, this works only when the furniture is arranged to permit an axis of movement that follows either a straight line or a smooth curve. Moving the end doors off center in Illus. 103 would not help because the axis is blocked by the furniture in the middle.

Adapting Proscenium Plans. The plans in printed plays show proscenium sets. Adapting these to a convertible proscenium set may present problems, but major alterations are rarely necessary. Even when they are, we can usually follow the printed design to some extent.

Printed plans are much less helpful to the arena designer. Drastic changes are almost always required. Indeed, if the captions of Illus. 102 through Illus. 106 did not identify the originals from which they were taken, you might not be able to tell which is which.

One reason for making changes is the fact that, even with makeshift seating, the designer cannot control the exact length of his walls. Thus, in Illus. 103, I would have preferred to put the end table beside the sofa at 1 o'clock instead of beside the chair at 2 o'clock, but the wall space did not permit this.

The set in Illus. 106 is an even clearer example. This is a raked version of Illus. 104, but the arrangement had to be entirely different because the walls are shorter. Also, I lacked room for a sofa at 5 o'clock and was forced to substitute a love seat.

Designs for proscenium interiors are usually controlled by the fact that wall space is limited. It must be used efficiently if each door and piece of furniture is to be worked in without interfering with sightlines. The arena designer faces the opposite condition. After he has located all the furniture in the printed plan, he usually discovers that one long wall is left bare.

Finding appropriate props to fill gaps in living-room sets gives me more trouble than anything else in arena design. Chairs, sofas, and tables are apt to look misplaced unless they are arranged in groups. The list of items that can be introduced or left out at will is extremely small. In fact, I have used up my entire list on the sets in Illus. 102 through Illus. 107.

Modified Arenas

Doors do wonders to make entrances and exits dramatic. Playwrights know this and often write scenes that depend on it. Stairs are also of great value in arranging interesting and significant movements and groupings. Arena sets have no doors. When stairs are available, they are in the aisles. This reduces them to a clumsy convention which may occasionally be required but which has no dramatic value.

These considerations have led many groups to adopt modified arenas, such as those in Illus. 108 through Illus. 110.

If we deepen the apron of a proscenium stage, it becomes a FORESTAGE. A plan of this type is well suited to the production of classic plays such as those of Shakespeare and the Greek playwrights.

When the main stage is shallower and the forestage is narrower, the result is called a THRUST STAGE (Illus. 108). It leaves room for doors and may permit stairs when the main stage is deep enough. Unfortunately, it raises serious directorial problems—especially when the forestage is deep and narrow. Thus, if character at B is afraid of one standing at A, the one at B would have to approach his enemy in order to exit. This is unnatural at best and can create an unwanted laugh if B tries to make it plausible by moving sidewise around A.

Illus. 109 places the audience on two sides and devotes the other two to scenery. Architects who like to appear advanced sometimes prefer this plan. As I have never worked on such a stage, I am not really qualified to comment. Nevertheless, it appears to combine the disadvantages of proscenium and arena stages without the virtues of either one. A corner stage might be set up in a gymnasium or armory and would serve well for a dramatic pageant. But I cannot see that a permanent theatre of this type has any merit.

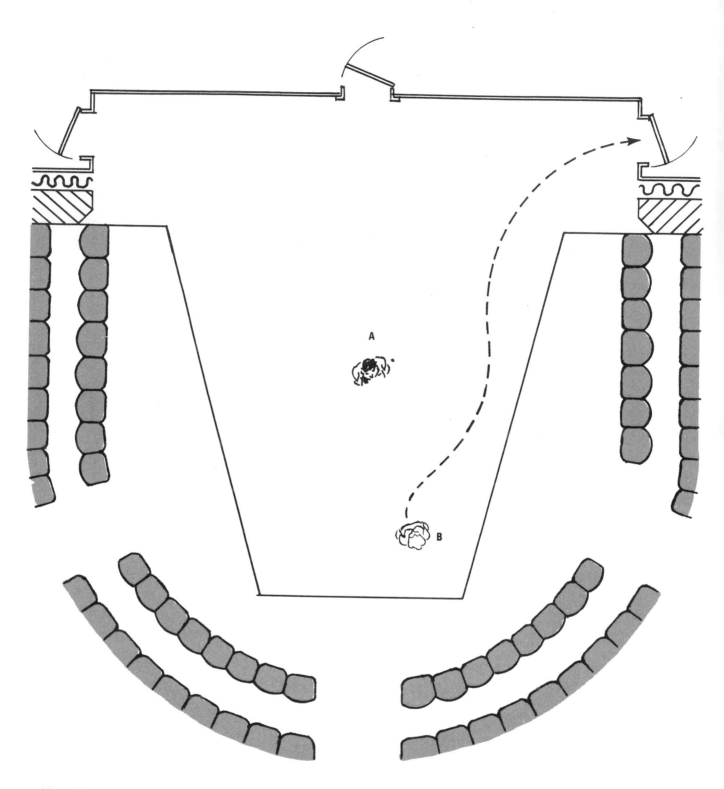

Illus. 108. THRUST STAGE. If the stage is a mere shelf like this one, and the forestage is deep and narrow, there is no room for furniture. Such a plan can also cause endless trouble for directors and actors. Thus, the movement shown would probably seem awkward unless the actor at A moves stage right. In many situations, it would be hard to find an excuse for such an action.

The double-ended arrangement in Illus. 110 is much more practical. It seats fewer people than either a pure arena stage or a thrust stage. On the other hand, it permits the use of a little scenery and lets the designer use doors and stairs. I know of no permanent theatre built on this plan, but I have found it highly satisfactory in a makeshift auditorium.

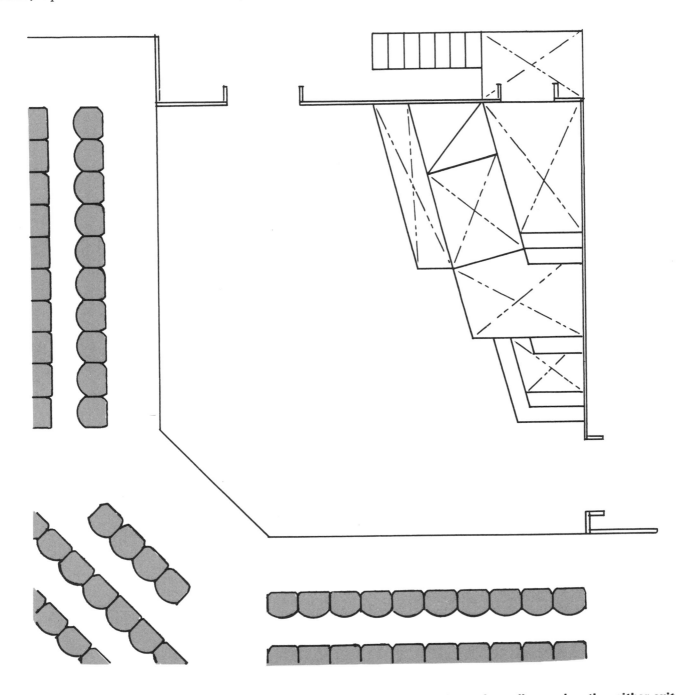

Illus. 109. CORNER STAGE. This plan almost forces actors to turn their backs to the audience when they either exit or mount the platforms. In most cases, such actions are technically bad. Note also that the convertible platforms in Illus. 68 (page 50) do not work well on a corner stage.

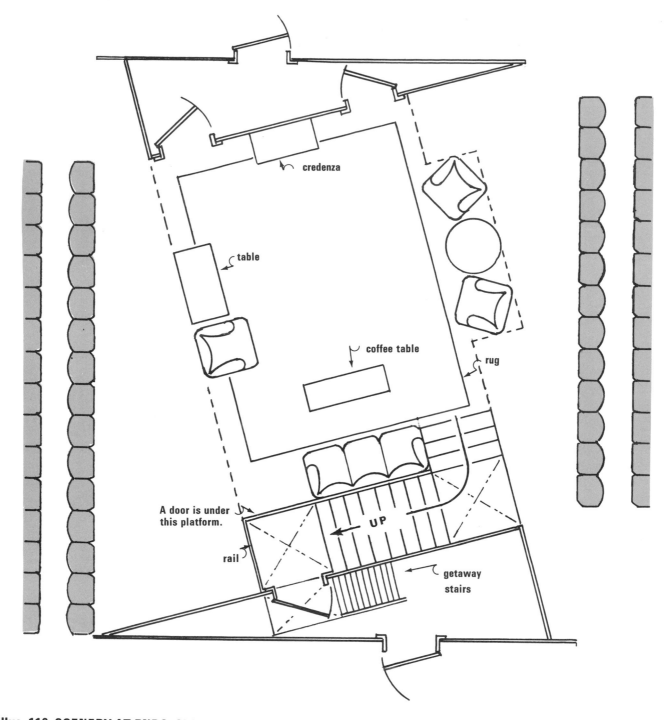

Illus. 110. SCENERY AT ENDS. Although this plan seriously limits the size of the audience, directors and actors will find it highly practical. Compare it with the arena version of the same set in Illus. 103.

INDEX